Doing Away With God?

Doing Away With God?

Creation and the Big Bang

RUSSELL STANNARD

Illustrations by Simon Jenkins

Marshall Pickering
An Imprint of HarperCollins*Publishers*

Marshall Pickering is an imprint of
HarperCollins*Religious*
Part of HarperCollins*Publishers*
77–85 Fulham Palace Road, London W6 8JB

First published in Great Britain
in 1993 by Marshall Pickering

10 9 8 7 6 5 4 3 2 1

Text copyright © 1993 Russell Stannard
Illustrations copyright © 1993 Simon Jenkins

The Author and Artist assert the moral right to
be identified as the author and artist of this work

A catalogue record for this book is
available from the British Library

ISBN 0 551 02770 3

Printed and bound in Great Britain by
The Guernsey Press Co. Ltd, Guernsey, Channel Islands

Contents

INTRODUCTION: GOD ON THE ROPES   1

1 BIG BANG CLUES   8

2 TELLING STORIES   17

3 BEGINNING AT THE BEGINNING   27

4 SO, WHAT'S NEW?   39

5 SOMETHING FOR NOTHING   54

6 PAY YOUR MONEY; TAKE YOUR CHOICE   61

7 THE THEORY OF (NOT QUITE) EVERYTHING   72

8 ANYONE AT HOME?   82

9 NOW THERE'S A FUNNY THING   89

10 HE WHO FIXED IT   98

11 GOD IN THE CREVICES?   105

12 DON'T TOUCH!   111

13 A SHIVER OR A CRUNCH   125

14 THE GURUS HAVE SPOKEN   132

POSTSCRIPT: TRUE, BUT IS IT NEWS?   144

INDEX   149

Introduction
God on the Ropes

God's been having a pretty rough time of it lately.

Take what happened the other day. The telephone woke me. It was a disc jockey from Radio Bedford. A disc jockey! Why would a . . .?

'I'm calling about the Big Bang – this latest discovery. They're saying it's the greatest discovery of all time. Any chance of you coming in to the studio this morning? You could tell us what it's all about and – what we really want from you: Does this still leave room for God? – that kind of thing.'

I struggled to wake up. What on Earth was the man talking about? What discovery? 'The greatest discovery of all time', and I'd never even heard of it!

'Sorry, what are you on about?' I asked in confusion.

'But you *must* know. It was on the news last night. It's in all the papers this morning – front page. "Scientists explain Creation." "Is this the end for the Creator?" That sort of thing. That's why we want to hear what you have to say – you being a scientist and a preacher and all that.'

'Well, you'll have to give me a minute. I was out last night. I didn't hear the news. And I haven't seen the papers yet. Ring back, will you – in half an hour, say?'

I hurried downstairs. How embarrassing. Professor of Physics at the Open University, and I have to learn about the most important physics discovery of all time from a local radio disc jockey! I collected the papers from the doormat, and returned to bed.

Sure enough, there is was, splashed across the front pages. I switched on the television. The news bulletins were full of it too. I studied the reports. Fortunately, both *The Independent* and *The Times* had fairly detailed accounts – all to do with a new observation made by satellite. It had cleared up a long-standing problem about the way the Big Bang developed.

But what had this to do with God? The discovery was telling us about the state of the Universe 300,000 years after the Big Bang. I ask you – *300,000 years after!* It had nothing to do with the actual act of creating the Universe. As for it being 'the greatest discovery of all time', come on – *really*!

I went on to read that the experiment had cost hundreds of millions of dollars. Ah, that explained it. When you've spent that much, it's important to reassure taxpayers that it's money well spent. I know; I've been involved in very expensive experiments myself. In Big Science it pays to take trouble over publicity. And – I had to hand it to these fellows – the hype for this discovery was fabulous. None of my experiments ever made the front page.

But as for belief in God, it had nothing to do with it, as far as I could see. So, that's what I decided to tell the disc jockey – it was not an angle worth pursuing.

But wait. If the disc jockey was confused, perhaps others would be also. So, when he rang back, I agreed to journey over to the studios in Luton. In between snatches of pop music, weather forecasts for the area, and news of traffic hold-ups, I dutifully reassured listeners that God was still alive and well – and moreover, was probably quite pleased that we now understood a little better how he got everything going.

Arriving home, I made a belated start on the day's work. I wondered whether it was in order to write and ask the radio station for travel expenses. Nobody had mentioned the subject, which I thought was a bit off. (It was all right – they did pay up!)

I was soon to discover that the disc jockey had not been alone in his worries. Directly after that broadcast, I received a call from Radio Oxford – the religious department this time. They too wanted my comments.

'I take it I'll get my travel expenses?' I enquired as a prudent precaution.

'How much will they be?' the voice at the other end asked.

'I don't know. But from here to Oxford and back must be 75 miles.'

'That much?!' he exclaimed.

'I'd do it just for the petrol,' I volunteered.

'Oh, I'll have to check with the producer. I'm not sure we have a budget for that sort of thing. This *is* a religious programme, you know.'

In the end we did the interview by telephone.

The following Sunday I was due to preach at my local church (I'm a Reader in the Church of England). Should I change the subject of the sermon and talk about this Big Bang stuff? I decided *not* to. Well, I get a bit self-conscious about being accused of giving 'physics lessons thinly disguised as sermons', even though it is meant as a joke – I think. Instead, I stuck to the theme for the day: 'Christ, the Bread of Life'. It was a normal, bread-and-butter type sermon (though perhaps without the butter?).

It was a mistake. Over coffee in the hall, I was deluged with questions about the Big Bang. Clearly, many had been deeply disturbed by what they had read. The unguarded comments of scientists and reporters ('God gets his P45' was how *The Mail* trumpeted the news) had caused untold confusion.

Two weeks later, I belatedly delivered the sermon about Creation and the Big Bang that everyone had been expecting of me.

LIONS 10, CHRISTIANS NIL

But even before I had a chance to deliver that sermon, God had got himself into more trouble. *The Observer* carried an account of a show-piece debate at the Edinburgh Science Festival. The headline declared:

'God comes a poor second before the majesty of science.'

The report stated that 'Richard Dawkins, the Oxford zoologist, inflicted grievous intellectual harm upon his opponent the Archbishop of York, Dr John Habgood.'

Apparently, Dawkins – who I know to be a brilliant expositor of science – had savagely attacked religion. He had likened God to Father Christmas and the Tooth Fairy. Habgood had been cleverly wrong-footed by Dawkins' opening approach, and was subsequently unable to rescue the debate. All this despite the fact that he was himself originally a scientist by training. I felt sorry for him; it must have been quite an ordeal. I continued reading the account: 'As one gloomy cleric uttered at the end of the debate, "That was easy to sum up. Lions 10, Christians nil".' In similar vein, *The Scotsman* gave as its verdict on the debate: 'God lost on points.'

I laid the papers aside and thought (somewhat apprehensively, I must confess) about an event that was due to take place in a month's time at the Royal Society. It would then be *my* turn to take on the formidable Dawkins in a debate entitled 'Has Science Eliminated the Need for God?' I do

sometimes wonder how and why I get myself mixed up in these things!

ENTER STEPHEN HAWKING ...

Yet more trouble: a TV documentary based on Stephen Hawking's *A Brief History of Time*.

How is one to fathom the phenomenal success of that book? Have you read it? I know you *bought* it (at least I presume you did – everyone must have a copy by now!), but have you *read* it? As far as I'm concerned, as a popular exposition of cosmology, it just doesn't work. In some places, where it deals with Hawking's own most recent ideas on imaginary time, for example, even professional scientists like myself have to struggle with it.

I sympathize with those publishers who were originally

offered the manuscript, and turned it down. I reckon I'd have done the same myself if I had been in their shoes. Which just goes to show how wrong you can be!

Someone once told me the secret of the book's success was the inclusion of the word 'Brief' in the title. There might be something in that, but I can't help thinking that's not the whole story. Clearly, there is an inherent interest in the subject itself. But more influential still, there's the paradox of finding one of the finest scientific minds of our generation locked up in a wreck of a body. What an extraordinary man Hawking is! No one could begrudge him his success.

But for all that, there's a problem: he is an atheist, and that is something that is widely known. Having described the Big Bang – and here one *does* mean the moment of creation, not something that happened 300,000 years later – he went on to declare in the television programme (as he also does in his book) that he could see no place for a Creator. When someone of Hawking's stature makes a statement like that, a shudder goes through religious circles at about level 8 on the Richter scale.

No, God's been getting a really bad press recently.

THE BOOK THAT BEGAN TO WRITE ITSELF

It was in the middle of all this, that I was contacted by the publishers HarperCollins:

'Would you write us a book?'

'What kind do you have in mind?' I asked.

'One aimed at reassuring those who feel threatened by science – a science they do not understand – a science that appears so often to undermine the self-respect of human beings – a science that scorns spirituality. Would you write it for young and old alike – for those who find the scientific ideas themselves hard to grasp, let alone their possible implications?'

I explained that the timing was all wrong for me. I was about to start work on another book – the third in the series of *Uncle Albert* books, aimed at explaining modern physics to children. It was true I did plan writing a popular book on science and religion, but that wasn't until 1998 – to coincide with a lecture series I was due to give at that time. Still, I said I would bear their request in mind, and if I thought of anything I would be in touch.

A few days later, I settled down at the word processor. Before me was the outline sketch of *Uncle Albert III* (or whatever it will eventually be called). I took a deep breath and prepared to tackle Chapter 1. But for reasons I still do not fully understand, what I typed began: 'God's been having a pretty rough time of it lately . . .'

1 Big Bang Clues

DETECTIVE WORK

So what is all this about a Big Bang? How can scientists possibly know that's how the world began – especially as it is supposed to have happened 15,000 million years ago?

Obviously there was no one around at the time, so there were no eye-witnesses. Instead, we must be prepared to do a bit of detective work. We must weigh up the circumstantial evidence – evidence based on clues that are still around today.

There are three major ones. They refer to three quite different phenomena, but they all point to the same conclusion.

FIRST CLUE: THE FURTHER, THE FASTER

Look up on a cloudless night, and what do you see? Stars. Tiny points of light. But they are not really tiny; they are huge balls of fiery gas – suns that are as big or even bigger than our Sun. They only appear tiny because they are a long way off.

There are about 6,000 visible to the naked eye. With the help of telescopes, more stars can be seen – fainter ones that are even further away. There are a great many of them; in fact, 100,000 million of them.

They are grouped together in a great swirling collection of stars shaped like a disc. This is the Galaxy. We are about two-

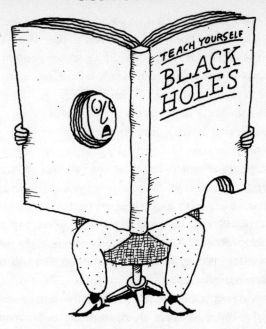

thirds of the way out from its centre. On a very clear night, away from the street lights, you can make out the Galaxy as a broad band of stars called the Milky Way. When looking at the Milky Way, you are looking at the Galaxy end-on – through the disc where the stars are densest.

Each star attracts each other star by the force of gravity. That is what keeps the stars of the Galaxy together and stops them drifting off into space.

If they all attract each other, you might wonder what stops them all landing up in a heap at the middle. The answer is that the Galaxy is rotating about its centre. Rotation tends to throw things off into space (recall what happens if a child on a roundabout does not hold on tight). The gravity force between the stars is used to counteract this 'flying outwards' tendency.

When I said there were 100,000 million stars, that was just for starters! Telescopes reveal not only the stars of our Galaxy, but at even greater distances, other galaxies. Each of these distant island galaxies has something like 100,000 million stars. In other words, just as our Sun is a very ordinary star, so our Galaxy is just a very ordinary galaxy. How many of these galaxies of stars are there? We believe there are 100,000 million galaxies – the same as the average number of stars in each!

If you find it hard to imagine what such huge numbers mean, don't worry. It's virtually impossible for anyone to grasp their significance. In this we are all reduced to the level of the primitive tribe whose counting system amounts to: *one – two – three – a lot*. With such numbers we have simply to accept them without trying too hard to visualize what they mean.

One important thing to find out about each newly discovered galaxy is how far away it is from us. The second is how fast it is moving.

Now you might think that the galaxies would be stationary – just sitting there in space doing nothing apart from slowly rotating about their respective centres. This is indeed what scientists themselves at first expected. But it turns out that this is not the case. The galaxies are moving – they are moving away from us. They are not drifting about at random, some moving towards us, others moving away. No. They are all moving away from us.

Not only that, but the further away the galaxy, the faster it is retreating into the distance – twice as far away, twice as fast; three times as far, three times as fast; ten times as far, ten times as fast . . . The furthest galaxies are travelling at incredible speeds – close to the speed of light itself, i.e. 186,000 miles per *second*.

It is the observation of the motion of the galaxies that provides the first clue about the Big Bang. Why? Because this is exactly the kind of motion one would expect if all the matter of the Universe had at one time been together at a point – and then exploded. Something coming out of the explosion twice as fast as something else would go twice as far in a given time; three times as fast, three times as far; etc – which is exactly what we find.

When did this great explosion take place? That's easy to work out. We know how fast the galaxies are travelling, and we know how far they have travelled (i.e. what their separation from us is). The sum is therefore no different from one like this:

> If a car is doing a steady 70 m.p.h. on the motorway, and it has travelled 140 miles, how long ago did the car start its journey? Answer: 2 hours ago.

In the case of the galaxies, the answer to the sum is that they started their journey 15,000 million years ago.

SECOND CLUE: UNWANTED BACKGROUND

With all that matter hurtling out from the explosion with such enormous speeds, the Big Bang must have been horrendously violent. This in turn makes us think that the matter came out hot. After all, just think of a nuclear bomb going off: matter thrown out violently, plus a fireball. This raises the question: Was the Big Bang also accompanied by a fireball?

In 1965, some scientists were trying to look at the radiation coming to us from the rest of our Galaxy and from other galaxies. But they picked up a background signal. Most annoying. Where was it coming from? It seemed to be coming from *everywhere*! It didn't matter where they pointed their telescope – at a distant galaxy, or at the empty space between the galaxies – the result was the same. It did not depend on the time of day, or the time of the year. Always the same infuriating, steady signal. The whole Universe was awash with this gentle heat radiation.

Then the penny dropped. What they had first regarded as a nuisance, turned out to be one of the most important finds of the century. Purely by chance, they had discovered the Big Bang fireball! Admittedly, it had nothing like the blinding appearance of the initial flash. 15,000 million years of wandering around the Universe had cooled it down. But the signs were unmistakable; there was no other explanation.

Mind you, there was something about this radiation that did *not* fit too well. It seemed to be *absolutely* uniform from all directions. To see why this was a problem, let's return to the galaxies.

As we've just noted, the Big Bang was hot – very hot. That means the matter came out as a gas. It could not have come out as solid lumps, because these would have been disrupted by violent impacts. After a while, when things had had a chance to cool down, gravity started to pull the matter together to form galaxies. How this actually came about we don't yet quite understand. Obviously, if the matter had been *absolutely* uniform, there would have been no reason why the matter would have clumped together in one place to form a galaxy in preference to somewhere else.

It would have been a bit like the proverbial donkey that finds itself absolutely equally placed between two identical piles of hay, one to its left, one to its right. It has to choose which one to go to. But there is nothing to choose between them. So what happens? The donkey starves!

If we are not careful, we are likely to find the same will be true of the matter in the early Universe. If each region in space is absolutely as good as any other for forming a galaxy, there's no reason why it should start forming in one place rather than another – so it wouldn't have formed at all. The material would have stayed in the form of a diffuse gas, progressively becoming more and more dilute as the Universe expanded.

So we have to say that the initial distribution of matter could *not* have been completely uniform; there had to be a certain lumpiness to it. From earliest times, there simply had to be regions of somewhat higher than average density, so that they could act as preferential centres of attraction. Once they started dragging in matter from the surrounding space, then there was no stopping the process. The matter dragged in increased the gravitational attraction, and that helped to drag yet more in. This then carried on until the Universe reached the state we see it in today: isolated islands of matter with virtually empty space in between.

Thus, one needs to have lumpiness on the scale that separates individual galaxies from each other. But more than that, there has to be a lack of smoothness on even larger scales. This is because one finds the galaxies themselves gathered together in clusters – several galaxies to a cluster. Next, one notes that the clusters form superclusters. Finally, on an even larger scale, one finds galaxies forming gigantic 'walls' of galaxies enclosing huge voids where there is essentially nothing.

The problem is how to marry together a fireball that was uniform throughout, with a distribution of matter that was anything but smooth – when both were supposed to have come from the same origin.

Enter the so-called 'greatest discovery of all time' mentioned in the Introduction. A study of the background radiation with *very* sensitive equipment – mounted on a satellite – revealed that the radiation was *not* absolutely smooth, as had been originally thought. It too showed irregularities. Moreover, these were on something like the scale of the irregularites in the distribution of matter.

So any lingering doubts that the matter of the Universe and the background radiation came from the same event – the Big Bang – were ended at a stroke. Hence the excitement surrounding that discovery.

THIRD CLUE: PREPARING THE INGREDIENTS

This concerns the *type* of matter to come from the Big Bang.

The matter we see around us consists of different types of atom. Each has its own characteristic nucleus, surrounded by electrons. The nucleus in turn is made up from two basic constituents: neutrons and protons.

The lightest nucleus is that of hydrogen; it consists simply of a single proton. The next heaviest is a rarer form of hydrogen called deuterium; it has a proton and a neutron. The nucleus of helium comes next; it usually has two protons and two neutrons, though there is a lighter version with two protons and only one neutron. And so on, all the way up to the nucleus of uranium, with 92 protons and 142 neutrons.

That is the situation as it is today: 92 different types of atom or element. But in the beginning it was not like that. At the extremely high temperatures that marked the initial stages of the Big Bang, not only were there no lumps of matter around, there weren't even any large nuclei. Any such nuclei would have been promptly smashed up into their component neutrons and protons. So, that's what one started off with: a piping hot soup of individual neutrons and protons, together with the electrons.

A few minutes after the Big Bang, the temperature cooled to a tepid 50,000,000,000 C (!). Now something interesting happened. A proton could ram into a neutron, and stick together to form the nucleus of deuterium. Because conditions were less frenetic now, there was a good chance that this composite nucleus would not get disrupted by future collisions. Indeed, there was now a chance that two deuterium nuclei would fuse to form the nucleus of the next heaviest element, helium. And so on.

But they had to get a move on. While this nuclear fusion was going on, the expansion of the Universe continued apace. The soup was getting thinner and thinner. As the density went down, there was less chance of the nuclei colliding and so less chance of the heavier nuclei being formed.

Not only that, the temperature was rapidly dropping. Once it went below 100,000,000 C, the nuclei, even if they did collide, did not have enough energy to fuse together.

So, after just a few minutes, the cooking of the nuclei petered out – leaving a 'freeze-out' concentration of the various elements.

Now, the exciting thing is that from a knowledge of the conditions of the Big Bang, it is possible to *calculate* what the final mix of the different elements ought to have been. It turns out that we expect 75 per cent of the mass to be in the form of hydrogen, and most of the remaining 25 per cent to be helium. There will then be just a little deuterium, lithium, etc.

How does that check out with what we observe today? We have to be a little careful. Subsequent to the Big Bang, there has been further cooking of the nuclei in the hot centres of stars. But when we look at the gas *between* the stars, and concentrate our attention on the abundance of deuterium, which is the least likely to have been affected by the types of fusion reaction going on in stars, the agreement with calculation is excellent.

CONSIDER YOUR VERDICT

So, there we have it: three independent pieces of evidence. All of them point to an explosive origin for the Universe. That is why scientists today are quite convinced of the correctness of the Big Bang theory – even though there were no eyewitnesses to the event!

2   Telling Stories

There's a great deal more to tell you about the Big Bang. But what I have said so far is enough for the time being – more than enough to worry quite a number of religious believers. 'What about Genesis?' they'll be asking. 'How does one square *that* with Big Bang theory?'

Some try to argue that there is no problem: that the Bible account of creation is *essentially* saying the same thing as the modern theory.

How they arrive at that view, I have no idea. We have, on the one hand, a progressive creation over a period of six days – a period which, according to biblical chronology, occurred some 6,000 years ago; on the other, an instantaneous creation 15,000 million years ago. In all honesty, we are dealing with two very different accounts.

And it's not just physicists who seem to be at odds with the Bible. What about biologists? According to them, the human race descended from the same ancestors as the apes – not from Adam and Eve. We are a product of evolution – a process through which more and more complicated and sophisticated forms of life gradually emerged over a vast span of time.

And this isn't just an idea. There's plenty of hard evidence to back it up. Not that the evidence is 100 per cent complete.

Tracing our ancestry back, we find gaps in the fossil records. But one should not make too much of that. The gaps are being progressively filled.

How far back does evolution go? Most biologists believe that it is only a matter of time before we shall be able to put together a plausible scenario for how all life evolved from chemicals – plain, ordinary inanimate chemicals.

Just in case you find that hard to swallow, let me point out that there appears to be no hard-and-fast dividing line between the living and the non-living. It all depends on how one chooses to define life. Generally one expects that a living thing will show various behaviour characteristics. But something like a modern-day virus exhibits only certain of those characteristics and not others. So, is it living or non-living? It's hard to tell; it's on the borderline.

That being the case, one can imagine the evolution of life

going right back to non-living origins – stretching back 4,500 million years to the chemicals lying around on the surface of the Earth soon after the planet was formed.

So what are we to conclude from all this? Have the cosmologists and the biologists combined to catch the Bible out? Is Genesis nothing more than a fairy tale?

FACT THROUGH FICTION

What I am about to say won't be to everyone's liking. But it can't be helped. The only sensible way out of this impasse, as I see it, is to accept that what we find in Genesis is not, and was never intended to be, a scientific account of our origins.

As with a book you might pick up at a library – whether it be poetry, history, romance, humour, biography, science – one has to read Genesis in the way it was *intended* to be read. One has to take the trouble to consider what the motivation might have been behind the writing of the book.

For example, one wouldn't dream of approaching a poem as though it were a scientific treatise – demanding evidence that an actual physical dagger pierced the woman's heart at the thought of her lover's betrayal. In the same way, one does not go to Shakespeare if one needs information about what Richard III was really like as an historical person.

The authors of such writings are just as much interested in *truth* as a scientist or an historian. But a different kind of truth – one that has to be approached differently. A truth about the nature and the experiences of people *in general*, perhaps – rather than what actually, physically happened to particular individuals.

Like many ancient civilizations, the Jews belonged to a story-telling culture. They passed on the fruits of their wisdom and experience in the form of easily recalled stories. It was a tradition that was to be perpetuated by Jesus with his parables. Whether, for example, there actually was a Good Samaritan is neither here nor there. What matters is what that story has to say about *us* – us as we are *today*.

Indeed, the practice of conveying truths through stories is one that flourishes even in our own times. One has only to think of stories like *Animal Farm* by George Orwell, or *The Lord of the Flies* by William Golding. Both have much to tell us about human nature. Even the facts of hard physical science can be rendered more palatable and easier to remember if they are wrapped up in a storyline (witness my own *The Time and Space of Uncle Albert*!).

These stories are all to be seen as vehicles for conveying truth. The fact that the stories do not refer to real events is of no significance – provided the reader is able to sort out the hidden truth from the storyline. Normally this is no problem. I find that 11-year-olds have no difficulty in disentangling Uncle Albert's thought-bubble, with its imaginary spacecraft, from the facts of Einstein's Relativity Theory that are revealed through them.

If only the same could be said of adult readers of Genesis today! Many resist any suggestion that one should treat Genesis as anything other than an absolutely literal account of what happened.

To some extent I can sympathize. Like any other devout believer, they rightly have an enormous regard for the Bible. If it is attacked, their natural response is to rush to its defence. And the defence is total; they are reluctant to concede an inch. After all, they argue, once one accepts that perhaps certain parts of the Bible are not literally true, where will it all end? One is on a slippery path to goodness knows where.

A PHONEY WAR

But *is* the Bible under attack from modern science? That's how some people like to put it. And certainly that's the angle the media push. Conflicts, fights and blazing rows are the stuff of journalism. But what is the true situation?

Firstly, when people say, 'The Genesis creation story has been caught out', which one are they referring to? There are two of them: the first is in chapter 1, the second begins at verse 4 of chapter 2. That straight away raises the question: Why two accounts – placed side by side, and contradicting each other?

The answer is simple: They are only contradictory if they are viewed as rival scientific accounts of our origins. This alone should alert us to the fact that they were never intended to be read in that way.

Secondly, we ought to ask how the people of the past viewed these writings. After all, they were living closer in time to when Genesis was written. They could have had a better feel for what was on the mind of the writers than we have today.

Going back to the early Christians, we find there were two schools of thought regarding how Genesis should be read. One was based at Antioch and tended to be literalistic in its approach. The other – the more influential – was based at Alexandria and treated the stories largely as allegory.

One member of this latter school was the third-century theologian Origen. He once said: 'What man of sense will suppose that the first and second and third day, and the evening and morning, existed without a Sun and Moon and stars?'

He clearly did not regard Genesis as literally true. He explained how the aim of the Holy Spirit 'is to envelop and hide secret mysteries in ordinary words under the pretext of a narrative of some kind and of an account of visible things'.

Then there was St Augustine, one of the greatest Christian teachers and theologians of all time. He wrote: 'In the beginning were created only germs or causes of the forms of life which were afterwards to be developed in gradual course'.

He wrote that 1,400 years before Darwin propounded his theory of evolution! Not that Augustine had any conception of the way evolution came about through the Darwinian idea of natural selection. But I suspect that had Augustine been around today, he would have had no difficulty in accepting our modern theory of evolution.

This, of course, raises an interesting question: If it was perfectly clear to most early Christians that Genesis was not meant to be a literalistic account of our origins, how come such an interpretation is so much in evidence today?

The strictly literalistic approach to the Bible came into the ascendency only at the time of the Reformation in the 16th century. It was a time of great upheaval. The Protestants were breaking free of the power of Rome. They put their trust in the Bible rather than in the Pope. Those remaining loyal to the Pope naturally wanted to reaffirm their own allegiance to the Bible. So, a situation developed in which the two rival factions sought to outdo each other in their professed loyalty to the Bible. That's how the idea formed that one should not in any way question what the Bible says. And from that time onwards, the literalistic interpretation of the Bible was handed down to the present time.

Thus, when believers today hold to a literalistic interpretation of Genesis, in the teeth of the evidence for the Big Bang and for evolution, they are not 'defending the Bible' – as they believe themselves to be doing. Instead they are defending a fairly recent – spurious – interpretation placed on the writings.

TRUTH WILL OUT

As for the 'secret mysteries' of the Genesis stories, what might these deep truths be?

* One God over all – the Creator of all there is.
* He takes a personal interest in each one of us.
* We are made in his image and have the potential to be God-like.
* We are by nature sinful and fall short of that potential and need his help.
* The sacredness of marriage (man and woman are one flesh).
* We are placed in this garden (planet Earth) to tend it and look after it.

Many more items could be added to the list . . .

What matters are these truths. People who come to accept them today through a literal acceptance of the stories are like those who heard the same stories long ago and likewise did not worry about scientific plausibility or historical fact. But that surely is not a satisfactory stance to take nowadays – not in the age of science.

And yet, what do we find? Far from the literalistic, fundamentalist wing of the church diminishing in influence, it is the one that is growing fastest. I must say this is a development I view with dismay.

Don't get me wrong. I am as happy as the next person in welcoming more and more converts to the faith. And there is no doubt in my mind that the relationship that my funda-mentalist friends have with God is absolutely genuine.

Indeed, I would go so far as to admit that to some extent I even envy them. They seem to me to have a simple, trusting, uncomplicated relationship with God, full of joy and exuber-ance. It certainly has its attractions – when contrasted with mine, say. My relationship tends to go to the other extreme – over-serious, constantly being worked at and agonized over!

But one thing I can say in favour of the type of relationship I have with God: it is one that welcomes and embraces the findings of science; it is not one that is compelled to reject them out of fear, or from a well-intentioned but misplaced sense of reverence for scripture. A proper sense of reverence for scripture? Certainly. But not one that is inappropriate.

The trouble with the literalistic approach is that I cannot see how it can be adhered to with any pretence at intellectual honesty. The scientific evidence is overwhelming. Surely God gave us our intellect to *use*, not to leave on the doorstep outside church. The truths of science are as much God's truths as any others.

I suspect that those who advocate the literalistic approach to the Bible, though making Christians of certain people, are at the same time causing untold harm to *others* – to those who feel drawn towards a religious attitude to life, but are repelled at the thought that they can only do this by blindly shutting their minds to the evidence.

Truth will out in the end. I know it doesn't always seem so. At the present time our culture appears to be going through a particularly bad patch of irrationality – witness the growth of New Age philosophy, interest in the occult, and the general backlash against science. But time will tell.

I earnestly look forward to the day when it will be generally recognized that one can take on board all the deep truths of the Genesis creation stories, *and in addition*, the scientific truths about God's world.

Then we shall see how God is revealing himself through this Big Bang world of ours. He is actually speaking to us through these scientific discoveries:

* The mind-boggling scale of the universe, for example, allows us to appreciate, to a degree never before possible, his awesome majesty and power.
* Through his willingness to work over a period of 15,000 million years to accomplish his purposes, we discern the extent of his patience and foresight.
* The fact that sophisticated life forms such as human beings can paradoxically develop and take shape from inanimate chemicals in a world where the overall tendency is towards decay and disorder, testifies to the sheer ingenuity with which he has devised the laws of nature.

No, there is no doubt in my mind that the findings of science should be embraced wholeheartedly by religious believers. That way we can learn even more about God, and more about ourselves.

ANYONE ELSE OUT THERE?

Before we resume our account of the Big Bang, I must address another kind of worry people have.

I've said that the immense scale of the Universe is to be seen as God revealing to us something of his power and might. That's true. But if the prime intention behind the Universe is that it should be a fitting home for human beings, doesn't the sheer size of the place seem a bit . . . well . . . over the top? A case of over-design, perhaps.

It depends how you look at it. The world started with a Big Bang. That means the expansion had to keep going for as long as was necessary for the evolution of intelligent life. And as we have seen, that is measured in terms of thousands of millions of years.

Given that the matter coming from the Big Bang had to resist the mutual attraction of the gravity between its components for this length of time (otherwise it would all have been pulled back together before evolution had done its job), it had to come out fast – close to the speed of light. The result? The Universe ended up big!

Mind you, I don't think for one moment that the human race on planet Earth is the only form of intelligent life in the Universe. The number of stars in the Universe, as we have seen, is vast. From what we know of the way stars form, we expect a high proportion of them to have planets. Many of these will be placed at a position relative to their local sun, such that they will enjoy a temperate climate, and thereby be conducive to the evolution of life.

On the assumption that life on Earth did not owe its origins to some absolutely outlandish freak of nature, the proliferation of Earth-like planets points to there almost certainly being other creatures in the Universe as intelligent as ourselves, if not more so.

This is one respect in which modern science can be thought to have enriched our understanding of our own place in the scheme of things. Presumably these other intelligent creatures rank as highly in God's estimation as ourselves, if not higher. But where's the harm in that? A bit of humility never did anyone any harm!

I am sometimes asked about the role of Jesus in relation to such forms of extraterrestrial life. I don't see a problem. In the same way as the Son of God came to Earth and took on the form of a man – the man Jesus – I see no reason why the same Son of God should not take on other forms for the benefit of life on those other planets.

3   Beginning at the Beginning

WOBBLY JELLIES AND RUBBER SHEETS

The impression I have given so far is that the Big Bang, apart from being the largest explosion there has ever been, was nevertheless an explosion much like any other. But this was *not* the case. The Big Bang was very special.

With any normal type of explosion, all the stuff starts off being concentrated at a point in space. When it goes off, the matter moves outwards from this point and progressively fills up the rest of the surrounding space.

In the Big Bang, all the stuff started off squashed together at a point. OK. But there was *no* space outside that point! What happened was that in the course of the explosion, *space itself* expanded. It expanded from a point to the enormous size it has today. In the process, it carried the matter along with it.

Crazy! How can *nothing* expand?!

The secret is that to a physicist, space is *not* nothing. Even what we call 'empty space' – the kind of space between the galaxies – is only 'empty' in the sense that there is no matter there (no stars, planets or gases). But that is not to say that it consists of absolutely nothing.

So, if it's not nothing, what is it?

I find it helpful to think of it as a kind of 'jelly' – a very thin jelly-like medium.

Calling it a 'jelly' has its problems. For example, with a proper jelly, you find it in the interior of a bowl, but when we get to the surface of the bowl, it comes to a halt – it has a boundary. From then on it's the glass of the bowl and not the jelly we find.

But with the jelly-like nature of space we have to think of the jelly as not only being inside the bowl, but also permeating *through* the glass of the bowl, and being *outside* the bowl – and everywhere else too.

Why think of space this way? Because space has properties, and these can differ from one point to another.

For example, the space close to gravitating objects, like the Sun or the Earth, behaves differently from the space further away. Close to the Sun, it behaves as though the jelly were a little thicker there. (It's a bit like jelly cubes not dissolving properly when you add the hot water; the undissolved lumps are thicker and more gooey.) This thickening of the 'space jelly' results in light travelling more slowly through these regions than elsewhere. It's similar to the way light travels more slowly through glass than through air.

One of the effects of this is that the paths of light beams skimming close to the surface of the Sun get slightly bent, much as they do when passing through a glass lens.

Another effect is that ripples can be sent out through space, as though someone were shaking the jelly about, causing it to wobble; these ripples are called 'gravitational waves'.

It is even possible to knock a hole in space! (The holes are known as anti-particles.)

The property of space that particularly interests us in connection with the Big Bang is that it stretches; it expands.

Stretching jellies are not too familiar, so let us switch to a different analogy: a rubber sheet. Imagine we have a rubber sheet with some coins stuck on it. Several people are asked to

get hold of the edges of the sheet and, on the word of command, they all pull – much like firemen holding a safety net ready for someone to jump. The sheet stretches; it becomes larger, and in so doing, the coins move away from each other.

If you were a little fly sitting on one of the coins, you would see all the other coins retreating from you. If you watched carefully, you would probably notice that the further away a coin was from you, the faster it was retreating from you.

Which, of course, is exactly what we find when we look through telescopes at the other galaxies; they are all retreating from us, and the further away they are, the faster they are moving. So the coins are like the galaxies. They are moving because the space between them (the rubber sheet) is expanding and carrying them along with it.

The rubber sheet is a good analogy, but like all analogies, it does break down. In the first place, it has people standing outside the sheet doing the pulling. But, as I have already mentioned, there is no space outside the 'rubbery space' of the Universe. Also, the rubber sheet has a centre which is equidistant from the points that mark its edge. But the Universe does not have an edge, as far as we know. So, it doesn't make sense to think of it having a central point either. It doesn't matter which galaxy you are on, all galaxies appear to be moving away from *you*. To all appearances, you seem to be at the centre of the Universe. The trouble is *everyone*, on *every* galaxy, thinks the same!

What all this means is that the instant of the Big Bang was not only the moment when the matter of the Universe was created; *it was also the instant when space itself was created*.

ANOTHER TIME; ANOTHER PLACE

That in itself is a remarkable idea. But the plot thickens! Perhaps even more remarkable is the notion that the Big Bang also marked the beginning of *time*. How do physicists arrive at *that* conclusion?

First, we have to appreciate the very intimate relationship that exists between space and time – a relationship revealed by Einstein's Theory of Relativity.

Now, don't get worried; I'm not about to launch into a long-winded explanation of the theory. But I do need to draw your attention to one or two of its results.

Imagine an astronaut in a high-speed spacecraft setting off from Earth to travel to a distant planet. After a certain time, he arrives at his destination. But after how much time exactly? It is found that the astronaut and the mission controller at Houston do not agree about the time of the journey. According to Relativity Theory, if the spacecraft travelled close to the speed of light (186,000 miles per second), the mission controller would find that the astronaut's clock would significantly lag behind his own. For example, at 9/10th the speed of light, the journey time as recorded on the astronaut's clock would be approximately *half* that recorded by the controller!

This effect, whereby clocks get out of step with each other, is one that affects *all* journey times – not just those undertaken in exotic spacecraft. For someone commuting to work by train, the journey time would appear less than it would for the wife or husband left at home. At train speeds, however – even Intercity train speeds – the effect is absolutely minute.

What we are talking about here is not something that affects only clocks. We are talking about *time itself* slowing down for someone who is moving. The astronaut's breathing, his pulse rate, his thinking processes, his ageing – they are all slowed down by the same factor.

Now, before you jump to the conclusion that high-speed travel holds the secret of eternal youth, two warnings:

In the first place, the effect, as I have said, is normally very small. A train driver would have to drive an Intercity express from London to Glasgow all his working life to gain one-millionth of a second on his stay-at-home wife. Hardly worth the bother, I'd have thought.

Secondly, because your thinking processes will have slowed down by the same factor as everything happening around you in your high-speed craft, you will not be aware that you are living longer. Which makes it all a bit pointless.

That is the first amazing consequence of the theory: the astronaut and the mission controller have different ideas about time.

The second is that they also disagree about the length of the journey, i.e. the distance from the Earth to the distant planet. At the same speed as before, 9/10th the speed of light, the distance for the astronaut is about half what it is for the controller.

If this is the first time you have come across this kind of thing, I can imagine your feelings. A bit unnerving, isn't it? Having spent my working life researching subatomic particles flying around at speeds close to that of light, these effects have long since become second nature to me. But I still vividly remember the shock and exhilaration of encountering Einstein's ideas for the first time as a student.

Take heart; it's not as chaotic as it might seem.

For instance, you might initially have thought that it would be easy for the controller to prove that it must be the astronaut's clock that had gone wrong – due perhaps to some malfunction arising from the acceleration, or something like that. All he would have to do is point out that, at the agreed speed of 9/10th the speed of light, the spacecraft could not possibly have travelled to so distant a planet in such a short time.

But wait. The astronaut does not agree about the distance travelled: 'Of course I only took half the time to do the journey,' he protests. 'It's only half as far as you are saying. What more do you expect?'

In fact, there is no way of proving who is right and who is wrong. There is no way of checking whether the astronaut's clock was *really* slowed down – as claimed by the controller, or, alternatively, that the distance *really* was short – as claimed by the astronaut. Both give equally consistent accounts of the journey. The only problem is that their accounts differ.

NOT GOING BY APPEARANCES

So how are we to cope with a situation where different people describe a situation differently? The answer is – in the same way as we normally deal with such situations.

Suppose I hold up an object, such as a pen, in a lecture theatre. I ask each member of the audience to describe what they see.

They all answer differently; no two people see exactly the same thing. Some think the pen looks long, others say it looks short, others (those who happen to be looking at it almost end-on from where they are sitting) might not be able to make out what it is at all.

Is this cause for concern? No. Why not? Because we realize that what the audience sees is not the object itself, but a *projection* of that object. Each person's eyes register a two-dimensional image projected onto a plane at right angles to the line of sight linking the pen to the eye. Because each member of the audience is sitting in a different position, each line of sight is different. Thus, each projection is different.

We don't worry about these 'disagreements' because we have got used to the idea that *appearances* can be deceptive. What matters is not what the pen looks like in two dimensions, but what it is like in three dimensions. On making allowance for how much the pen lies *along* the line of sight, i.e. along the third dimension, there is no problem. Each person has a different two-dimensional projection at right angles to the line of sight, but also a different one-dimensional projection along the line of sight. If each person combines their own respective differing projections, *they all end up agreeing on the length of the pen in three dimensions*. Hence, no confusion.

So it only remains to regard that pen as an analogy for what happened during the interplanetary journey. As regards that journey, there are two items to focus our attention on: the event marking the departure from Earth, and the event marking the arrival at the distant planet. As we have noted, the astronaut and the controller differ about both the separation in time between those two events, and also their separation in space.

Now suppose – just *suppose* – that we did not live in a three-dimensional space but a four-dimensional one. Moreover, suppose that the mysterious fourth dimension had something to do with time. I know that sounds odd; we experience space and time in such different ways; it is virtually impossible to imagine what kind of connection there could be between them. But, as I said, just suppose.

We could then work out the separation of the two events in this four-dimensional spacetime. We do it, and what do we discover? The astronaut and the controller *agree*!! They get exactly the same answer for the separation of those two events in four dimensions. And what applies to this particular journey, applies to all situations. Regardless of which pair of events we think of, regardless of how fast people move, or in what direction, or where they are situated in space, they all agree on the separation between two events in four-dimensional spacetime.

This being so, physicists have come to accept that reality is actually four-dimensional. What we perceive directly – spatial distances and time intervals – are but appearances. They are 3-D and 1-D projections respectively of something that is really 4-D.

Now for goodness sake don't try to visualize a 4-D object. It will only give you a headache! Our brains were never meant to perform such a feat. As far as visual pictures are concerned, by the time we have the three spatial dimensions (up-down, left-right, backwards-forwards), there's nowhere left to go! But the mathematics of Relativity Theory (the calculation of the 4-D separation) guides us to the truth.

It is a little like a pilot landing his airplane in a fog. He would *like* to be able to see the runway with his eyes – but he cannot. Instead, he must allow his instruments to lead him home. It is only when he safely touches down that he knows this was the right thing to have done.

Summing up, we find that time is much more like space than we might have thought.

This is not to say that there is *no* difference between the two. Not only do we measure them with different types of instrument (a clock in one case, a ruler in the other), but we move forwards in time, not backwards – unlike space, where we have the freedom to move in any direction.

Also there is an asymmetry to time that is not shared with space. For example, with two photographs of a cup, one showing it whole and the other smashed on the floor, we instantly know which one came first (i.e. the order in which to place the photographs along the time direction). But we do not know in which direction the cup handle points (it could equally be pointing east, west or any other spatial direction).

So yes, there are differences between time and space – as we always thought. But there are also astounding similarities and an inescapable interconnectedness between them.

It was Einstein himself who once remarked that it was now more natural to think of physical reality as 'a four-dimensional existence instead of, hitherto, the evolution of a three-dimensional existence'. So, space and time become seamlessly welded together. There can be no time without space; there can be no space without time.

THE TIME THAT HAD NO 'BEFORE'

The significance of all this for our understanding of the Big Bang can now be made clear.

Earlier, I said that the Big Bang marked the creation of space. But now we have learned that space and time go together; they cannot be separated. Conclusion? The Big Bang must also have marked the beginning of time itself! It was not a case of 3-D space coming into existence at some point in time. That would have meant that there would have been time before the Big Bang. But time could not exist before the Big Bang if there was no space to go with it. There was no 'before'. Whether we like it or not, we have to bend our minds around the idea of 4-D spacetime being created as a totality.

That is one way in which 'time before the Big Bang' becomes a meaningless concept. But there is possibly another. It is a suggestion proposed by Stephen Hawking. It goes something like this:

As we go back in our imagination towards the time of the Big Bang, conditions get more and more extreme. The density of matter increases. All the matter of the Universe is squashed down to a volume the size of the Earth, then to the size of a house . . . the size of an orange . . . a pea . . . a pinhead . . an atom. . . a nucleus . . . Eventually it ends up at a point. At that stage the density of matter becomes infinite.

Now there is no way our understanding of physics can handle a situation like that. What has been found in the past is that, as one has explored ever more extreme conditions, the laws of physics, as they were understood at the time, broke down. New laws had to be proposed – laws that not only could handle the old situations, but could also take on board the new. Relativity Theory was a case in point; it was able to deal with everyday situations, just like the old laws it supplanted, but on top of that, it could also cope with conditions of extremely high speeds.

So we expect our current laws to break down just before we reach the point of infinite density. What will happen then? That's anybody's guess. Here is Hawking's fascinating suggestion:

Remember how I said that in Relativity Theory we have to think of time as much more like space than we might otherwise have guessed – and yet there remained differences that allow us to distinguish the two? Well, Hawking's idea is that as one gets very close to the point of infinite density, something peculiar happens to time. It begins to lose those characteristics that mark it out from the three spatial dimensions. Instead of a 4-D spacetime, with three spatial axes welded on to one time axis, we end up with a kind of 4-D space, where there is nothing particular to distinguish the time axis from the other three.

This being the case, as we go back in time towards the instant of the Big Bang, we might discover that time gets so mixed up with space that we never actually get to the Big Bang! We never quite reach the boundary of existence because we get 'diverted'.

Help! An analogy to the rescue:

This time I want you to imagine that you are travelling along a road running due south towards a seashore that extends east-west. You are 60 miles from the sea, and are travelling at a steady 60 m.p.h. Carry on like this and you will get very wet exactly one hour from now. Forty minutes later you pass a sign saying '20 miles to the sea'; you reckon twenty minutes to splash-down. Later still a sign saying '10 miles'; ten minutes to go. Then 'one mile'; one minute to go (inflate water wings!).

But one minute later, there is no splash; ten minutes later, still nothing has happened; you are still driving along the road. What has happened?

Near the anticipated end of your journey, the road began to develop a bend. Gradually, without you realizing it, you were progressively changing direction. Though for most of your journey you were going due south, heading straight for the sea, right towards the end, you began to veer to the east. Long after you should have reached the brink, you are cruising along a road that has become the coast road.

That's how it is with time – if Hawking is right. As you imagine going back in time, you reckon 15,000 million years and you get to the instant of the Big Bang – and go out of existence. But it might not be like that. In the closing stages of that journey into the past, you might discover that time somehow changes direction – you never quite get to that boundary of existence.

This, then, is a second way in which there might be no time before the Big Bang. Instead of time coming to an abrupt halt at the boundary of existence (going out with a Bang), it might simply melt away (going out with a whimper).

4 So, What's New?

THE OUT-OF-WORK GOD

It's time to take stock again. What are we to make of these latest thoughts on the Big Bang? What is their significance for religious belief?

Hawking's own reaction is to dismiss the idea of a Creator. Either the Universe did not have a beginning, in which case there is nothing for God to do, or if it did have a beginning, there was no time before the Big Bang in which he could do it.

CREATING TROUBLE

When talking of God as Creator, we are speaking metaphorically. There's probably no other way to talk about God other than through metaphors and analogies.

We do it, for example, when we speak of God as our Heavenly Father. Here we focus attention on the fact that our relationship to God is similar to that of a child to an earthly father.

But in talking about God in this way, we must be on our guard. There has to be a point where the analogy – *any* analogy – breaks down. We have already seen this happening when we've used analogies for explaining abstract physics ideas (recall how the rubber sheet had a midpoint and an edge with space outside it – which proper space does not have). The same is true of analogies that try to throw light on the nature of God.

In calling God 'Father', for example, the analogy breaks down over the issue of sex. An earthly father is male – obviously; but in calling God 'Father', we do not imply that he is specifically male. To do that would be to rob ourselves of the insights that come from regarding him also as our Heavenly Mother. Then why not call God 'Mother'? Why not indeed. Except that by making a big issue over deliberately switching to calling God 'Mother' – after all this time calling him 'Father' – one perhaps ends up paradoxically drawing attention to the sex question, rather than the reverse. Either way we can't seem to win.

We have to use the same caution over calling God 'Creator'. To some extent it is a good analogy. I certainly think it's helpful, but perhaps that has something to do with my hobby: sculpting.

I know scientists have a reputation for being philistine when it comes to the arts, but in my experience nothing could be further from the truth. Many of my physicist colleagues are musicians, and, as I say, I enjoy sculpting. It's an activity that reaches the parts that my science and my writing don't! Whenever I get fed up with work, I make for the backyard and my latest sculpture, and within minutes I am lost in an entirely different world.

What I find fascinating about making a sculpture is the way it takes on a life of its own. Although it is all my own work, somehow it evolves its own personality. A two-way interaction is set up.

I might start out with a pretty good idea of how I want it to look. But then the sculpture itself seems to take over; to some extent it ends up differently. When it's finished, there it stands over against me - an object distinct from myself. And yet with something of me in it; though true to its own self, it expresses something about me.

I sense this is how God the Creator must feel about his Universe.

Then there is the question of scale. Earlier I said how God reveals something of his majesty through the sheer size of the Universe. Well, I also get a kick out of making sculptures that are large. There is something thrilling about relating to a sculpture that is your own size or even a little larger. The first time I did a large one, I felt self-conscious. There was no way I could hide something that big from the neighbours! Now I just accept their puzzled looks. (Professors are supposed to be a little eccentric anyway, aren't they?)

So, the analogy of God as a Creator is a good one – in several respects. But that should not blind us to the fact that, pressed too far, the analogy runs into trouble.

For instance, when I engage in sculpture, all I am really doing is rearranging materials: expanded polystyrene, plaster, drain-pipes, car-body underseal, Isopon filler, shellac and bronze powder. All the materials are available; I simply have to go along to the DIY shop and buy them.

God, on the other hand, creates from nothing. That's the first difference – and quite a difference too!

But there is another. It arises directly out of what we learned about the nature of time in that last chapter.

When I set about a sculpture, I first get an idea; then I make a decision as to when I shall start work on realizing that idea; finally comes the activity itself.

But that is not how it can be with God. As we have seen, there is no time before the Big Bang. Therefore, the notion of God sitting in splendid isolation, getting the bright idea that it might be nice to have some people to relate to, then starting to create the Universe as a home for them – none of this will do. There was no time in which he could lay his plans. And, if Hawking's speculation is correct, there was not even a 'start' to the Universe.

KEEPING IT GOING

Hawking comments on this in *A Brief History of Time* as follows:

> Most people have come to believe that God allows the universe to evolve according to a set of laws and does not intervene to break these laws. However, the laws do not tell us what the universe should have looked like when it started – it would still be up to God to wind up the clockwork and choose how to start it off. So long as the universe had a beginning, we could suppose it had a creator. But if the universe is really completely self-contained, having no boundary or edge, it would have neither beginning nor end: it would simply be. What place, then, for a creator?

This is the much-quoted passage that so worries religious believers. But what does it actually amount to.

It appears to be a dialogue, or confrontation, between science and theology – with theology coming off a poor second. But is it a fair contest? In the red corner, we have science as represented by one of the finest scientific minds of our generation; in the blue corner, we have what 'most people' think about God. But is that the way to conduct a dialogue between science and theology? How would it be if we were to match a professional theologian against what 'most people' think about science? Most people are perfectly capable of going through life with little or no knowledge of the finer points of either theology or Einstein's Theory of Relativity.

No. If we are to have a proper dialogue, we need to listen to experts on *both* sides. When we do that, a very different picture emerges.

We do not even have to call on twentieth-century theologians – those benefitting from up-to-date scientific knowledge. The seemingly revolutionary idea of there being no time before creation is not in fact new. Fourth-century St Augustine got there before twentieth-century physicists! (Good old St Augustine – again. That man would have got a Nobel Prize had he been around today.) Augustine held that God was responsible for the existence of absolutely everything – *and that included time.* Given that time is a feature of this world, it must have been created along with everything else in the world. The fact that such an idea was current so long ago makes it clear that, for early Christian thinkers, God the 'Creator' must have been a pretty sophisticated conception.

Contrary to what 'most people' are supposed to think, the Christian conception of God is not one in which he merely lit the blue touch-paper and retired. Christian teachers from earliest times have been careful to maintain that, linked to the idea of God the Creator, is the companion idea of God the Sustainer. In other words, creation is not to be thought of as a one-off activity – something confined to an initial phase (whether that be thought of as a six-day period, an instantaneous Big Bang, or an initial Hawking-style stage in which time progressively assumes its now distinctive form). God's power is needed to *sustain*, or to hold, everything in existence.

Again we are in danger of pushing an analogy too far. When we think of something being sustained we might have in mind, say, footballers sustaining their effort until the final whistle. The players work successively from minute to minute to keep up the pressure. But it's not quite like that when we think of how God sustains the world. Unlike the footballers, he is not confined to a particular instant of time, moving successively from one to the next. We have to think of him somehow approaching the time axis from a lateral direction.

A lateral direction? What does *that* mean?! Another analogy:

Imagine some matchboxes stacked on top of each other to make a tower. The tower stands because the table top pushes up on the bottom box; that box passes the thrust on to the second box; the second box then in turn pushes up on the third, etc.

That's one way of keeping the boxes from falling through the table top.

The other is to lay the tower on its side. Now the table top pushes up on all the boxes *directly* – rather than have each box passing on the thrust to its neighbour.

Whereas with the tower upright, one of the boxes – the bottom one – played a crucial role (remove it and the tower collapses), with the tower on its side, all boxes are now on a similar footing – the first box in the sequence is no longer special.

God's sustaining power is a little like the second of these two arrangements. He acts directly on *each* instant of time, rather than on just one. That way nothing special hinges on the initial instant. Indeed, if Hawking wants to remove that instant altogether, why shouldn't he?

So, speaking of God as Creator, what we mean is that his creativity is at work everywhere and at every instant of time.

He is the fundamental, underlying reason why there is something rather than nothing. He was, and is, and will be the ground of all being.

TRACKING GOD DOWN

What other thoughts arise out of the cosmology we learned in that last chapter?

Do you recall the Russian astronaut coming back from his space trip and declaring that he had not found God up there? How seriously should we take such a remark?

It is not difficult to understand how people reading the Bible can get the idea that God and his Heaven are 'up there'. After all, Moses went up a mountain to get closer to God, and Jesus is described as *ascending* to Heaven. But are we meant to take such references literally? Did the ancient Jewish people *really* believe in a three-tiered universe – a cosmology rooted in the Babylonian idea of a flat Earth, Hell down below, and a hemispherical dome above, beyond which there was Heaven?

Every schoolchild today must surely have heard of the trouble Galileo got into with the church over the way he championed the theory that it was the Earth that went round the Sun rather than the reverse. But not many people stop to wonder why it was that the view being defended by the church at that time was *not* the traditional biblical three-tiered universe. Instead, it was Aristotle's idea of a *spherical* Earth surrounded by concentric spheres that was being supported.

The switch from the Babylonian cosmology to the Greek one had happened by the eighth century. What is interesting is that this was accomplished without the slightest fuss or scandal. This alone seems to me to indicate that the idea of a Heaven being literally 'up there' might never have been taken all that seriously by the early Jews and Christians. How else are we to understand how the metaphor of Heaven 'up there' got replaced by one based on Heaven 'out there' – without anyone being hauled up before the Pope?

All of which goes to show that whatever the row over Galileo was about, it was *not* cosmology – not really. In fact, the whole unfortunate episode arose from the Pope feeling betrayed and insulted by the way his former friend Galileo had chosen to represent his own views about cosmology. It was a silly, personal squabble – not the big science versus religion debate it was later cracked up to be. (This is a subject I have dealt with at length in an earlier book, so I'd rather not go into here again.)

God 'out there' rather than 'up there'. Can we do any better than that? With the help of Relativity Theory, I reckon we can.

In seeking the whereabouts of Heaven, we are trying to locate it somewhere. Our instinctive idea is that it must be found at some particular position in three-dimensional space.

But now we know better; we recognize that we live not in a 3-D space, but a 4-D spacetime. The reason it took so long to make the connection between space and time, is that we experience the fourth dimension in a different way to the other three.

Now, this raises an interesting question: Are there yet more dimensions – a fifth, a sixth etc. – dimensions that are experienced in yet other ways?

Physicists have in fact been trying out just such ideas. A theory currently being explored suggests that space might be ten-dimensional! Where might those extra seven spatial dimensions be? Under our very noses – all curled up tight, instead of being stretched out like our customary three spatial dimensions and one time dimension. These extra dimensions

might be perceived in the form of such things as electric charge.

Could it be that there are dimensions we do not experience *at all*? Could there be dimensions that accommodate Heaven? Why not?

None of which, of course, proves that Heaven is located in some extra dimension. I merely mention this possibility as an illustration of the way in which questions related to God can sometimes take totally unexpected turns.

All of which makes the comment of the Russian astronaut, about not finding God up there, sound more than a little naive.

LOOKING INTO THE FUTURE

Before returning once again to the Big Bang theory, let us briefly reflect on something else we discovered in that last chapter.

Recall how Einstein told us that we need to deal with a four-dimensional reality, not a three-dimensional reality evolving in time. Let's be clear about what this means.

It is saying that our 4-D spacetime cannot evolve in time because time is not something separate from it: time is incorporated into the spacetime *itself*.

This faces us with one of the most curious features of spacetime: it never changes; it just sits there – doing nothing. All of space is there – *but so too is all of time*.

Just imagine: the whole of time – what we call the past, the present and the future – it is all there. Every instant of time is there on an equal footing with every other instant. *On an equal footing*. I mean that.

'But,' you might protest, 'what about the instant called "now"? That surely is special.'

Strange as it might seem, physics recognizes no unique instant called 'now'. It treats the instant we choose to call 'now' in *exactly* the same way as any other.

And if it has no way of distinguishing the 'now' – the instant dividing the past from the future – then it also can take no account of terms like 'past' and 'future'. 'Earlier times' and 'later times'? Yes. But such terms apply to *every* instant along the time axis; every instant has times that are earlier or later than itself.

The whole idea of an absolute past, consisting of fixed events that used to exist but do so no more, and an absolute future, consisting of uncertain events that do not yet exist – all this is entirely foreign to the notion of a four-dimensional existence. I repeat: according to Relativity Theory, *all* of time exists.

I asked you just now to imagine all of time just sitting there. I'm sorry; that was not fair. No-one can imagine such a strange state of affairs.

To do that you would have to imagine that in this room where you are reading this book, there exists not just what is happening now, but also you *starting* to read the book, and you *finishing* your reading of the book. There exists what was here before the house was built, together with what will be here after the house has been demolished and replaced by something else.

Really! How can one imagine *that*? Our conscious perception is so overwhelmed by the immediacy of the present, our experience so dominated by the impression of the everchanging flow of time, that we instinctively rebel against the static conception of 4-D spacetime.

Just like you, I rebel against the idea. I can't help it. And yet, as a physicist, thinking like a physicist, I have of necessity to accept that, *in some sense*, it is true.

Now you might think that something this strange and alien must be quite new and unprecedented. But no. Religious thinkers were treading paths like this long before the physicists. In the Bible one constantly comes across strange references to time:

* Jesus, for example, declared, 'Before Abraham was, I am.' An interesting use of tenses?
* In speaking to Martha, Jesus makes clear that eternal life is not something one has to wait for as an 'afterlife': 'I *am* the resurrection and the life,' he says. Note: he does not say, 'I *will be* the resurrection and the life.' Eternal life – that which is beyond time – is to be found also in the midst of this temporal life. For this reason, at the Holy Communion service we are told, 'The Lord *keep* you in eternal life,' not 'The Lord bring you to eternal life.'

Next, we note references to God's foreknowledge:

* Peter saying to the crowd, 'This man was handed over to you by God's set purpose and foreknowledge . . .'
* Peter addressing his first letter to 'God's elect . . . chosen according to the foreknowledge of God the Father'.
* Paul writing to the Romans, 'For those God foreknew he also predestined to be conformed to the likeness of his Son.'

The idea that God knows what each of us will do, even before we have made up our minds what to do, has never been easy to accept. If God knows the future, does that not make a nonsense of free will – a concept surely vital to our understanding of ourselves in relation to God?

Many people, including not a few professional theologians, find the whole idea of the future being fixed and already known to God so distasteful that they deliberately downplay the importance of such biblical references.

But what we now discover is that much the same kind of problem has surfaced in physics. Although as conscious human beings, we live out dynamic lives that are constantly evolving and changing in response to the way we exercise our freedom of action, physics is telling us that all the instants of our lives from birth to death somehow exist alongside each other. The whole sequence of life is etched into the fabric of four-dimensional spacetime.

That being so – with the future apparently fixed – again we ask, what does this mean for free will?

Whether we are thinking on the basis of God's foreknowledge or Einstein's 4-D spacetime, I do not myself see free will threatened. The analogy I find helpful is the following:

I am watching a TV broadcast. The manager of the England football team is being interviewed. The reporter is taking him to task about yet another boring, uninspiring performance.

The manager stoutly maintains that he is not in the slightest bit disappointed; he reckons the boys played really well, and we have to realize that these days there are no easy matches. 'You would say that, wouldn't you,' replies the interviewer. And so it goes on.

Watching this interview, I find myself caught up in the cut and thrust of it all. I find myself feeling sorry for the grilling the manager is getting. But I worry that if he really believes what he is saying then he's not likely to be seeking improvements. I wonder whether he is just putting on a brave front, and can't wait to get back to the dressing room to give the boys a roasting.

The interview ends. Cut to studio. It is only now I discover that we are in the middle of a news broadcast. What I had been watching had not been a live broadcast, as I had supposed. It was recorded earlier in the day. While I had been caught up in what was being shown – the interview as it was progressively developing and getting more and more sticky for the manager – the whole interview from beginning to end already existed; it was there on videotape in the studio. Whereas I could experience that interview only a little at a time in strict sequence as it was broadcast, the newscaster had access to all of it. For me it was uncertain what the speakers would choose to say next. For the newscaster there was no uncertainty; he had access to the full contents of the videotape; he knew infallibly what followed each and every incident shown.

Does that mean that as far as the newscaster is concerned he is watching automatons? Of course not. The videotape is still a record of people doing what people normally do – making decisions and exercizing free will.

I see God in relation to time something like that. He is able to look down on time – all of it – from some privileged vantage-point outside of time, just as the newscaster was able to access any part of the whole tape.

The analogy is, of course, a crude one. It is easy to see where this one breaks down. Unlike God, the newscaster is *not* outside time. He has to wait until the interview has been recorded, and then, only *after* the event, is he able to assume his God-like perspective. But I think the analogy does contain a little insight.

Especially is this so when one further elaborates it. Our life, as etched into the fabric of 4-D spacetime, is the equivalent of the videotape – one that God can take in at a glance, even though we are confined in consciousness to but a tiny part of it. But what I have not yet told you is that this is no ordinary videotape. It is God's home video. By that I mean that God is one of the characters featured on the tape. We are to think of God in one sense as looking down on the totality of life, upholding it in existence. In this sense he is beyond time. But in another sense God is right here *in* time; we interact with him; he speaks to us; we speak to him; we meet him in Jesus Christ. So we are to see God's action etched also into 4-D spacetime. This is the mystery of how God can be both in time and outside of time.

As I indicated, nothing of this is easy to take in. In the deepest sense there is mystery here – meaning that there is something about it that will forever lie beyond our full grasp.

When it comes to thinking about such matters, I reckon myself lucky to be a physicist. I probably have less difficulty accepting God's foreknowledge than most people. After all, the biggest hurdle is acceptance that the future is there to be seen. As far as that is concerned, I *know* in my professional capacity that it must be so. That being the case, all God has to do is to find a way of looking at it. I shouldn't have thought that would have been too much of a problem for him!

5 Something for Nothing

A DO-IT-YOURSELF UNIVERSE

Recently there has been the startling suggestion that perhaps the world made itself. It all happened spontaneously; it did not need anyone to intervene and make it happen. This is seen as yet another attack on the notion of a Creator God.

Normally one thinks of the laws of physics as telling us how the world behaves. They allow us, with considerable confidence, to trace back what was going on right up to a tiny fraction of a second from the Big Bang itself.

However, it has always been thought that the actual instant of the Big Bang itself was beyond their reach. There was no way the laws could handle the situation where the density of matter was infinite.

This remains true. And yet, that does not necessarily prevent the laws from explaining why there should have been a Big Bang of some sort. Accordingly, the laws would not only tell us how the world behaved from a fraction of a second after the Big Bang to the present time, they might also be capable of explaining how there comes to be a world in the first place.

THE ULTIMATE FREE LUNCH

When it comes to creating a universe, there are essentially two hurdles to overcome. The first is how to get something for nothing. That is not as difficult as one might suppose.

Take, for example, the creation of electric charge. There is clearly a lot of electric charge in the world. But electric charge comes in two forms – positive and negative. There is positive charge on the nuclei of the atoms that make up the world, and negative charge on the electrons that surround the nuclei. There is no difficulty creating electric charge. In high-energy physics laboratories, where I used to work, we do it as a matter of routine. The trick is to create more than one charged particle at a time – one with positive charge, the other with negative. Thus, the *net* charge remains zero.

How much *net* electric charge is there in the universe? The answer, very precisely, is *zero* – the positive and the negative types exactly balance each other out.

Next, we look at momentum. This is a property possessed of moving objects. It depends on how heavy the object is, how fast it is going, and in which direction. It's a measure of the ability of the object to barge other things out of its way.

If, from a stationary position, I start moving, I acquire momentum; new momentum comes into existence. But in order to get going, I have to push with my feet against the floor. That gives the Earth an equal and opposite momentum. We don't see it flying off in the opposite direction because it is so much heavier than I am. But it does acquire a tiny, tiny motion away from me – sufficient to give it the equal and opposite momentum. So, as with the electric charge earlier, a positive is balanced out by a negative.

There are as many things moving in one direction as there are moving in the opposite; the Universe as a whole is not moving in any particular direction. Thus, the net momentum in the Universe, like the net electric charge, is zero.

Next we consider angular momentum; that is a property of rotating objects. If I start rotating on the spot, like a spinning ice-skater, I acquire angular momentum. But in order to start turning, I again have to push against the ground. This gives a twist to the Earth – an additional angular momentum in the opposite sense. Again there is a cancellation.

There are as many things in the Universe spinning one way as the other; the Universe as a whole is not spinning. So, the net angular momentum is zero.

But what about matter? Can this, in some sense, cancel itself out too? Here we must turn again to the Theory of Relativity – in particular, to the equation $E = mc^2$.

Everyone has heard of this equation, but what does it *mean*? One of the important things it means is that matter, or mass, m, is a locked-up form of energy, E.

Energy comes in many guises: heat, kinetic energy, gravitational potential energy, electromagnetic energy, etc. Thanks to Relativity Theory we now recognize that matter is also a manifestation of energy.

Normally it remains locked-up or frozen-in. But under special circumstances a fraction of it can be released. This is what happens in nuclear bombs and in the Sun. Under the specially hot conditions one gets in those situations, collisions take place between the nuclei in such a way that if one were to gather up the pieces after the reaction, some of the matter would be found to be missing – the matter would weigh less than it did at the start. Why? Because some of it had been converted into other forms of energy: heat and light.

Now the interesting thing is that, like electric charge, momentum and angular momentum, energy can be both negative and positive. Negative energy manifests itself whenever two objects are bound together.

The Sun and Earth, for example, are bound by their mutual gravitational attraction for each other. They have energy – the energy locked up in their matter. If the two could be separated by being pulled apart, they would still have the same amount of locked-up energy as before. But in pulling them apart, energy has to be given to the system. Where has it gone? It has been used to overcome or cancel out the negative energy the system had when the two bodies were bound.

So in the normal situation of bound bodies, the total energy consists of the positive energy locked up in the matter, together with the negative gravitational energy. In other words, the net energy of the bound system is somewhat less than that of the separated system.

This immediately raises the interesting question of how much net energy there is in the Universe.

Clearly, when one looks at all the stars in the Universe, there must be an absolutely vast amount of positive locked-up energy. But think: there is also a lot of gravity in the Universe. The Moon is attracted by the gravity of the Earth; the Earth is attracted by the Sun's gravity; the Sun is attracted to the other stars that make up the Galaxy; the Galaxy is attracted to the local group of galaxies; the local group is bound to a supercluster; the supercluster experiences the gravity of other superclusters.

So, how much negative gravitational energy is there in the Universe? The amazing answer is that there is enough to cancel out all the positive locked-up energy of matter. In other words, the net energy/matter in the Universe is zero.

Thus we see that many of the most important prominent features of our Universe can be reduced – in net terms – to nothing.

This is not to say that we have reached the point where we can demonstrate that *every* property cancels out. Indeed, according to the way we currently formulate our theories, they do not. But we know enough to suspect that when we reach a final formulation of the laws of physics, defining properties in a way that suits that formulation, we would not be surprised to learn that the Universe adds up to precisely NOTHING. Albeit, an ingenious rearrangement of nothing!

ROULETTE PHYSICS

Which brings us to the second problem involved in having the Universe create itself: how to bring about the ingenious rearrangement of nothing.

Again, this does not seem to be an insuperable problem – judging by the way some scientists speak. They simply put it down to a *quantum fluctuation*. What is meant by *that*?

When we learn physics at school, we are taught that everything that happens must have a cause. Cause is followed by effect. Stone flying through the air towards window – cause; window shattering – effect. That effect then becomes the cause of the next effect – boy sent to bed early. So on down the causal chain.

Given the first cause, one can predict what the effect will be, then in turn predict what the effect of that will be, etc. Everything down the line becomes predictable – at least in principle.

With the advent of quantum theory all that changed. Now we know that from a given state of affairs, one can only predict the probability of a *variety* of possible later states. Repeatedly setting up the identical initial state will lead to *different* end results: a 60 per cent chance of one, a 30 per cent chance of another, a 10 per cent chance of another, for example. And that's all that can be determined beforehand: the *relative probabilities* of the possible outcomes.

If this is the first time you have come across this, I can well imagine your feelings. How could one possibly live in such a chaotic world? The answer is that the quantum uncertainties involved are normally very small – certainly as judged on the scale of phenomena we are used to dealing with in everyday life.

Take, for example, the normal errors of judgement involved in returning a tennis ball across the net. Even for a Wimbledon champion, these are huge compared to the additional inherent quantum uncertainties. The latter are completely masked. Quantum uncertainties only really come into their own once one gets down to the subatomic level – the realm of the very small. The smaller the objects concerned, the larger and more unpredictable the fluctuations can become.

So, what has this to do with the creation of the Universe? Simply this: the Universe itself started off very small. In fact, infinitesimally small. Such a tiny region would be subject to huge quantum fluctuations – as large as you like.

Thus comes the suggestion that in the beginning, there was an initial state of nothing. There was a small but finite chance that this would be succeeded – via a quantum fluctuation – by a state consisting of something. That something was the Universe. As soon as the Universe popped into existence, it promptly underwent a Big Bang.

That, then, is the proposal. It sounds quite attractive.

Which is not to say that it is free of difficulties. A quantum fluctuation? *What* – precisely – undergoes this fluctuation? It is not at all clear. Normally quantum fluctuations occur at certain positions in spacetime, but there was no spacetime to begin with.

Secondly, quantum physics is normally applied to the behaviour of component parts of the Universe. It does not follow that the same theory can be applied to the Universe as a whole.

Still, it is an interesting suggestion – one that deserves attention.

6 Pay Your Money; Take Your Choice

METHOD IN THE MADNESS

So, would a do-it-yourself Universe get rid of the need for a Creator God? Could the laws of physics have produced the Universe on their own?

Let's think for a moment about these laws. A remarkable feature of the Universe, but one easily overlooked, is that it is law-like; it is intelligible.

At first sight it doesn't seem that way. We appear to live in a mad world of bewildering complexity and variety: hundreds of thousands of different chemicals; vast numbers of species of animals and plants; ceaseless, ever-changing patterns of movement.

And yet, strange to say, behind this richness and diversity there lies breath-taking simplicity and order.

Matter is made up of atoms. There are only 92 naturally occurring types of atom. As we have seen, these consist of a central nucleus with electrons buzzing around it. The nucleus is made of neutrons and protons which, in turn, consist of even smaller constituents: the quarks. So, all those different chemicals eventually reduce to just a few basic constituent particles – quarks and electrons. Each of these is point-like; they have no internal structure. They could not be simpler.

Next, add a few forces: gravity, the electrical force, the

magnetic force, a nuclear force that binds the atomic nucleus together, and a weak force that causes some radioactive nuclei to explode. That's all.

Except that it is not even that many forces. Maxwell showed that the electric and magnetic forces are simply different manifestations of the one force: the electromagnetic force. And in our own time it has been recognized that the weak radioactive type of force is just a different manifestation of electromagnetism. So currently we are down to just three forces. Who knows, perhaps the time will come when we shall discover that these three can be whittled down to a single force.

So, just a few types of particle, subject to just a few types of force, behaving in a regular, reproducible manner according to the laws of nature.

And just as there are few particles and few forces, there are also only a few laws of nature. Could it be that one day we shall discover that these seemingly different laws are but different manifestations of a single law? Everything governed by one law? That would be tremendously exciting and aesthetically pleasing.

In fact, physicists are so excited at this prospect, they have given this hypothetical, all-embracing law a name – the Theory of Everything!

Whether it will turn out to be that simple we do not yet know. It might, of course, be a case of counting chickens before they're hatched! But we hope not. What we *do* already know is that the cosmos is run according to very few laws.

All this bewildering variety of nature that confronts us – it can be understood; it all makes sense. It can all be worked out – with a bit of intelligence.

Presumably it didn't have to be that way. It's easy enough to imagine a world where anything and everything could happen – a complete free-for-all where nothing was predictable. If that had been the case, we probably would not have been here to see it.

But that still leaves the question of why the Universe has the form it does. Why is the Universe of a type that allows intelligent life forms to develop in an orderly manner to the point where they can ask such questions?

WHO MAKES THE RULES?

Which brings us to the crucial question: If it takes intelligence to understand the Universe, did it not take an Intelligence to put it in place originally?

It is all very well saying that the Universe came spontaneously into existence through a quantum fluctuation, but why a *quantum* fluctuation? Where did the law of physics governing the process come from? Did it require some Intelligence to devise it? And why should it have been *quantum* physics rather than some other type of physics? Did an Intelligence have to make a choice as to which kind of physical world it should be?

A WORLD THAT HAD TO BE?

Those determined not to let God get a look in pin their hopes on an extreme version of the Theory of Everything (ToE) idea.

They hold that when we get to the ToE we shall at that stage be able to recognize that it was the *only* type of theory there could have been. There will be something about it that will show how the Universe is the way it is because that is the only kind of universe that is feasible.

If this extreme version of ToE were to be vindicated, there would be no need to invoke a supreme Intelligence to make a decision; there would simply be no decision to make.

UGH! MATHS!

To examine whether there might be any substance to this claim, we begin by noting that the underlying language of physics is *mathematics*.

Now, I know many people react in fear and dread at the very mention of the word 'mathematics'. Perhaps you are one of them. Well, I promise you there is nothing to worry about; I am not about to throw equations and formulae at you, or anything of that sort. All I want to do is talk a little bit *about* mathematics. (If this does not reassure you sufficiently, you can always skip to the summary paragraph at the end of the chapter. But I hope you will give it a try; I think you'll find it quite interesting.)

So, what do we mean when we say that the underlying language of physics is mathematics? We mean, in the first place, that physical concepts can be quantified – we can put a number on them.

That in itself is quite surprising. After all, the same is not true of mental concepts. I might say that I feel more depressed today than I was yesterday, but I cannot say that I am three times as depressed now as I was then. I can say that deciding to get married is a big decision; choosing which pair of socks to wear is a small decision. But is the marriage decision 100 times, 200 times or 1,000 times as big? Trying to put a figure on it does not make sense.

And yet when it comes to physical concepts, putting a figure on it makes perfect sense:

* 'This weighs 3.4 times as much as that.'

* 'Yes, officer, but I was only doing 75, whereas that Jag must have been doing 100.'

Not only can physical concepts be quantified, there are rules for deriving the values of those quantities from the values of other quantities:

* 'If a room is 12 feet long by 9 feet wide, it will need 12 square yards of carpet.'
* 'According to the astronaut, travelling at 9/10th the speed of light, the distance from the Earth to the distant planet will be approximately half what it is for the mission controller.'

So, mathematics deals in numbers and ways of relating those numbers according to certain equations, or formulae. How it comes about that the physical world lends itself to such a description is deeply mysterious.

In saying that the world can be described in mathematical terms, I should perhaps make it clear that it is not a case of saying: 'Over here is the world, and over there is mathematics, and – wow, how about that! – they match.'

No, there are many forms of mathematics – in fact, an infinite variety of them. It is a question of discovering which particular form of mathematics matches up with what goes on in the world. The quest is to find the appropriate mathematical structure.

That being the case, there are already certain things we can say about the ToE – even before we discover what the theory is! This arises because there are certain *general* conditions governing the properties of mathematical structures. *All* mathematical structures – including whatever structure is relevant for describing the cosmos – *must* obey these general conditions. So, what are these conditions?

Before talking of them, I should perhaps make clear what I mean by a mathematical structure, and how it is possible to have different types of mathematics.

To set up a mathematical structure, one has first of all to choose a set of assumptions. These are called the *postulates*. For example, before a start can be made on geometry, we have to make clear what our underlying assumptions are. These will include such things as:

* A straight line is the shortest distance between two points.
* One and only one straight line can be drawn between any two points.
* Two straight lines can intersect at one and only one point.
* Through any point outside a straight line, one and only one perpendicular can be drawn to the given line.

On the basis of these postulates, one can then trace out the various consequences that flow from them. This brings us to the second feature of the mathematical structure: the *theorems*. The famous Pythagoras' Theorem is one of the consequences that come from adopting the geometrical postulates.

The complete structure, therefore, consists of the underlying set of postulates, and erected upon them, the various consequences or theorems.

With regard to the mathematical structure that describes the cosmos, the postulates would correspond to the laws of physics, and the theorems to all the motions and possible events that occur in the Universe as a result of the operation of those laws.

COMMON SENSE – THAT ISN'T

Now the important point is the following: A general property of mathematical structures is that, from within that structure, there is no way of justifying the initial choice of postulates – they are simply *given*.

But, you may object, that can't be true, can it? Surely the postulates are *obvious* – they don't need justifying. Take those we have just been talking about: the definition of a straight line in terms of it being the shortest distance; only one straight line between two points; two straight lines intersecting at just one point; etc. How could things possibly be otherwise? It's nothing more than common sense.

No, it isn't. The geometry we described above may be the one we all learned at school – what we call Euclidean geometry – but it does not apply in all circumstances.

Suppose, for example, we were interested in the geometry that applies to the surface of a sphere, such as the surface of the Earth. The shortest distance between two points on that surface (assuming we are allowed to move only over the surface and not burrow through the Earth) is the line we would get by stretching a rubber band between the two points. In other words, the 'straight line' for spherical geometry would be the arc of a great circle (a great circle being a circle with its centre at the centre of the Earth). I know it's odd to have to think of a 'straight line' as being the curved arc of a circle, but this is simply how we are *defining* a 'straight line' for the purposes of doing geometry over the surface of the sphere.

That's fair enough. But note what happens to the other postulates. Suppose one wanted a 'straight line' from Greenwich to Accra in Ghana. Both lie on longitude zero, and we know that a line of longitude is a great circle. So all we have to do is travel due south from Greenwich. That way we trace out the 'straight line' between the two points.

But note, that is not the only option. We could, if we so wished, have gone due north, carried on round the other side of the globe and still ended up at Accra, having kept to the same great circle. In other words, there are *two* not one, 'straight lines' joining those two points. This means that for spherical geometry, the second of our postulates would have to be replaced by some other.

The same goes for the other postulates. For example, note that the Equator, like the lines of longitude, is a great circle, and so qualifies as being a 'straight line', but it intersects each line of longitude in *two* places, not one.

So, Euclidean geometry does not apply to the surface of a sphere.

'Big deal!' you might be thinking. 'Who cares about geometry on a sphere – unless you happen to be a navigator? It's geometry in three-dimensional space that matters, and the postulates for that are obvious.'

I'm afraid they're not. Strictly speaking, the postulates given above do not even apply to ordinary three-dimensional space! That might come as a surprise to you; it certainly caught the scientific community by surprise when Einstein first proposed it.

According to his General Theory of Relativity, gravity affects the properties of space. It does so to the extent that 'straight lines' are no longer what we would think of as straight. A 'straight line' (meaning the shortest distance between two points), when passing close to the rim of the Sun, has a kink in it! And this has subsequently been verified experimentally.

Why am I saying all this? Simply to underline the fact that there is nothing obvious, or commonsensical, about any of the postulates of geometry. There are an infinite number of possible geometries, each underpinned by a different set of postulates. It is the job of the physicist to investigate – *experimentally* – which is the appropriate one for describing the state of affairs we find in the world.

What applies to geometry, will apply equally to the mathematics underpinning the Theory of Everything. If we ever do discover such a theory, there will not be anything obvious or commonsensical about it. One will not be able to look at the underlying postulates of its mathematical structure and say, 'Of course. It's that way because it could not have been otherwise.'

Why? Because we ourselves belong to that Universe; we are described *within* that mathematical structure. And we know that from within a mathematical structure – *any* mathematical structure – there can be no justification for the original choice of postulates. Those postulates – and the ToE to which they relate – will remain for all time as simply *given*.

But given by *whom*?

MORE LOOSE ENDS

In fact, for those who subscribe to the over-optimistic (not to say arrogant) extreme view of the ToE, the situation is even more hopeless than that described so far.

One has only to refer to the work of the mathematician Kurt Goedel. He discovered a second general property of mathematical structures – one that places even tighter bounds on what one might hope to demonstrate mathematically, and hence in our present context, what the ToE might be able to say.

Goedel was able to demonstrate that for many branches of mathematics it was not possible to prove the *consistency* of the mathematical structure. This means that if one arrives at a particular theorem, or consequence, from the given set of postulates, it is impossible to prove that one could never arrive at a contradictory conclusion by arguing from the postulates by a different route.

Either that, or, if one *can* prove that the postulates are consistent and no contradictory conclusions will arise, then it can be shown that there will be true statements about the mathematical structure that can never be *proved* to be true. With such statements, no matter how many times they are tested experimentally, they are always vindicated. And yet – infuriatingly – we can never uncover *why* this should be so.

In other words, what Goedel was able to show was that mathematics is afflicted with a fundamental lack of completeness – it has untidy loose ends that cannot be got rid of. And this in turn means that the final formulation of physics – written as it will be in a mathematical language – will also be afflicted by an intrinsic lack of completeness. Which is, or *should be*, a salutary thought for all physicists.

IN SHORT . . .

Summarizing, we can say that the Universe might well have come into existence spontaneously from nothing – via a quantum fluctuation – but question marks remain:

* How should we interpret the intelligibility of the laws that govern the Universe? Do these point to an intelligent source?
* How do we account for the laws being these quantum laws, rather than some others? Did it take a supreme Intelligence to decide?

7 The Theory of (Not Quite) Everything

When scientists speak of the 'Theory of Everything', they are expressing the hope that one day they might be able to reduce physics to a single law. ToE simply refers to *physics*.

But I doubt that that's what most people think. Garbled newspaper reports can all too easily give the impression that scientists really are on the verge of explaining everything – absolutely *everything*. A chilling prospect.

This belief is reinforced when Hawking, in referring to the 'complete theory' in *A Brief History of Time*, describes such a prospect as 'the ultimate triumph of human reason – for then we would know the mind of God'.

Walk into a bookshop these days and what do you find? Titles such as *The Mind of God* by Paul Davies, and *Unravelling the Mind of God* by Robert Matthews – all spawned from Hawking's catchy phrase.

Most people, of course, will not be buying these books to find out what they are actually about. But they do see the titles – blazoned in big letters across the dust-jackets.

So, what are they to think? Scientists have succeeded in getting God sorted out? They have triumphed where theologians down the ages have failed? Concepts such as 'love' and 'salvation' have now been incorporated into a formula?

And what of the scientist himself? If, by his scientific investigation and assessment, the totality of God's mind can be laid bare, where does that place him in relation to God? Science becomes the religion, the scientist the high priest – or even the god, perhaps.

I'm sure it was never the intention of these authors to promote such a triumphalist view of science. Yet it is a view that some people do hold.

THE TAKE-OVER BID – THAT FAILED

Extravagant claims on behalf of science are nothing new. Some fifty years ago, a view was pushed that there was no other route to truth than that offered by the scientific method. For something to be worth talking about, it had to be open to scientific investigation. A statement was to be regarded as meaningful only if it could be experimentally verified.

The Verification Principle, as it came to be known, proved very influential. One of its effects was that, at a stroke, it killed off God. After all, there are few who would claim that God's existence was something that could be scientifically verified. One certainly could not *force* a sceptic to believe by the sheer weight of the evidence.

Today, most professional philosophers – including some of those who earlier were among its strongest advocates – dismiss the Verification Principle as old hat. It has been thoroughly discredited.

To begin with, it soon became apparent that the principle's underlying assertion – that only statements open to verification are meaningful – could not *itself* be verified! Not exactly a promising start.

In response to that, the principle was reworked. In its revised form it read: Only statements that can be verified are scientific statements.

Note that what we are now talking about is what constitutes a *scientific* statement, rather than a *meaningful* one. This backtracking allowed certain non-scientific statements to be meaningful once more – something that sensible people had not doubted for one moment!

But that was not the end of it. The philosopher, Karl Popper, next showed that in a sense one never actually verifies the truth of a scientific statement or law. No matter how many times experiments come up with results in agreement with the proposed law, there is no way to guarantee that it will always be like that. There will always remain situations where the law has not been tested, and that is where it might break down.

The history of science is full of examples of this. As we have already seen, the kind of physics that went unchallenged for 300 years, and is still taught in school, is now known not to hold at high speeds (where relativity takes over), nor in the realm of the very small (where quantum theory holds sway).

So Popper was led to propose that the Verification Principle should be replaced by a Falsification Principle. According to this, a scientific statement was to be defined as one that could, in principle, be *falsified*. As he pointed out, what experiments *can* do, is come up with an unexpected result that shows that the proposed law is *wrong*.

In other words, science can never prove that it is right; only that it is wrong. What a climb-down!

Even that was not the end of the story. It was later realized that even proving a law false might not be all that straight-forward.

Take what happened over the law of conservation of energy. This is a law that sits at the very heart of physics as we understand it. It is believed that energy is always conserved. It might appear under different disguises – energy of movement, or heat, or negative gravitational energy, or locked-up energy in matter – but the sum total of energy never changes.

Then along came radioactivity. In a certain experiment, a subatomic particle blew up. When the energy was counted up afterwards – the energy of movement and the locked-up energy in the bits left over from the mini-bang – it was found that some was missing. The total did not tally with the locked-up energy in the original particle. So, what should one conclude?

According to the Falsification Principle, one ought to abandon the law of conservation of energy. Is that what the physicists did? No. They *believed* in the law; they had *faith* in it. In the teeth of the evidence, they clung to the seemingly discredited law.

Belief? Faith? Surely that's what you get with religion, not science?

Belief and faith are indeed part and parcel of the fabric of religion. They are in evidence when, for example, a Christian remains committed to the idea of God as a God of Love, even in the face of examples of human suffering that are hard to reconcile with such a view. It is not that the Christian wilfully believes *anything*, regardless of the evidence. It is just that the idea of a loving God is *so* central to the whole system of religious belief – in so many other ways it has tremendous explanatory power – that one is prepared to live with the seeming anomaly.

But this is what happens in science too. Over this matter to do with radioactivity, the law of conservation of energy was so central to physics – it had proved its value in so many other ways – that physicists were prepared to ignore the dictates of the Falsification Principle, and simply live with the seeming anomaly.

In the event, their faith in the law was vindicated. It was later discovered that among the debris coming out of the mini-bang was a hitherto undetected particle – the exceedingly elusive particle known as the neutrino. It was this particle that had been carrying off the missing energy.

Thus, having replaced the Verification Principle by one

based on the opposite idea of falsification, we have now to recognize that even this much watered-down statement looks a bit shaky.

A LITTLE HUMILITY?

Why have I taken the trouble to tell you the chequered history of the Verification Principle?

Because the insidious influence of this principle lingers on. Though it should have been buried long ago, it still keeps raising its ugly head. It makes its presence felt whenever someone is moved to make some outrageous claim on behalf of the supposedly all-conquering, all-knowing methods of science.

Echoes of it are also there whenever someone declares that they are perfectly prepared to take religion seriously – provided that it can be *proved* to them that God exists. Underlying this demand is the assumption that claims regarding God's existence – like everything else – are suitable objects for scientific scrutiny.

Now, I would not like anyone to mistake what I am saying. This has not been an attack on science. How could it have been? I love my physics. I wouldn't spend so much of my time trying to interest children and laypeople in the subject, if I did not. It is the supreme method for tackling many important questions affecting life and experience.

What I *am* attacking are the overblown claims so often made on behalf of science – claims that science is the sole arbiter on *all* matters.

The truth of the matter is that science engages in only a *limited* field of study. Never lose sight of that. And even within those narrow confines, it is not as sure-footed as most people think.

TO BE OR NOT TO BE

What might those limitations – those confines – be?

For a start, science cannot say what anything *is*. That's right. At a fundamental level, it cannot say what anything actually *is*.

That might strike you as incredible.

'Surely', I hear you say, 'You have yourself already given the lie to that by stating on a number of occasions in the book what certain things *are* – what their nature is. Take matter, for instance. You said that matter is made of atoms; an atom is made of a nucleus and electrons; the nucleus is made of protons and neutrons; and protons and neutrons are made of quarks. So, everything is made of electrons and quarks. So, there we have it. What *is* matter? It's a pile of electrons and quarks.'

But does that *really* tell us what matter is? No, not at all. We haven't said what quarks and electrons are – other than that they are point-like somethings.

There are, of course, additional statements we can make about them. We can say, for example, that each electron and quark spins about its axis like a top. But that still does not throw light on the nature of the 'stuff' out of which the tiny top is made.

Or we can say that the particles carry electric charge. But that only gets us into deeper water still. It raises the question: What *is* electric charge? Again, we can't actually say.

We introduce the notion of electric charge because it helps us to understand the movement of the particles better. For example, it is noticed that when two electrons are placed close to each other, they tend to try and move away from each other. Why do they do that? We say that they each carry an amount of negative electric charge, and that like charges repel each other. Good. That explains the motion of the electrons. But it does not tell us anything about what electric charge *is* – any more than it helps us to understand what the matter is that carries the charge.

Talking about motion brings us up against yet more unknowns. The motions are in space and time. But what actually *is* space? What actually *is* time? We know how to measure them. We can assert that this distance here, called a metre, is 100 times that one, called a centimetre; or that an hour is 60 times as long as a minute. But the actual nature of space and of time? They remain a mystery.

So, if science is fundamentally incapable of explaining what anything actually is, what *does* it explain?

It describes how things *behave*. That's all science ever does. It describes how point-like objects behave in space and time – and it manages to do that without ever coming clean about the nature of the 'stuff' that makes up either the objects, or the space, or the time. Put that way, it can sound a pretty modest enterprise!

WHY, OH WHY?

Another limitation is that science is interested only in questions beginning *'How . . .?'* How things behave. It has no way of tackling questions that begin *'Why . . .?'* It cannot, for example, answer the question: 'Why is there a Universe rather than nothing?' Nor has it anything to say about: 'Why is the Universe the way it is rather than some other way?' All it can talk about is *how* the Universe behaves.

Whereas the restriction on not being able to answer questions about what things are might be regarded as mildly frustrating, this latest restriction is crippling. It means that science is quite incapable of tackling questions to do with meaning and purpose.

In one of the earliest, and still one of the best, accounts of the Big Bang – *The First Three Minutes* – Steven Weinberg, having splendidly described the physics, permits himself to wax philosophical in an Epilogue. There he makes a statement that has since been often repeated: 'The more the universe seems comprehensible, the more it seems pointless.' He continues in this mournful vein by speaking of human   life as 'a more-or-less farcical outcome of a chain of accidents'.

But for someone locked into an exclusively scientific way of looking at things, how could it be otherwise? Science is *exclusively* concerned with 'How?'-type questions. Having had the 'Why?'-type questions ruled out from its remit, one must not be surprised to find that science on its own appears to suggest that the Universe is pointless!

It is at this juncture that religion has its contribution to make. Religion is specifically concerned with the 'Why?'-type questions.

Those who cling to science as the *sole* arbiter on questions – in all fields – have only one way out where 'Why?'-type questions are concerned. Not being part of the scientific endeavour, they must be ruled out of court as meaningless. They are not proper questions. They are on a par with questions such as, 'Have you stopped beating your wife yet?' (Assuming, of course, that *is* a meaningless question!)

Now it may well be that questions of purpose are indeed meaningless. But they certainly sound pretty meaningful to me. Not only that, they sound a lot more *important* than the 'How?'-type questions.

As human beings, there's no getting away from the fact that we have to be concerned about the basic mechanics of *how* to live our lives – in respect of getting enough to eat, some place to sleep, avoiding danger, etc.

But that's surely only part of it. There can be few people who live out their lives as though they had no aims or purposes whatsoever. And if it is meaningful to ask low-level questions of purpose, such as:

'Why did you leave the light on?'
'Why was he so rude to me?'
'Why are you moving to London?'

then why not the higher-level questions, such as:

'Why are we here at all?'

To rule out such questions simply because science is not equipped to handle them, smacks of arbitrary high-handedness.

8 Anyone at Home?

There is one further way in which science is limited. It is so important that I thought it best to devote a chapter to it. It's to do with the fact that the physical sciences have nothing to say about the existence of minds.

Brains? Yes. Science can describe the physical structure of the brain, the various chemicals out of which it is made, how they are situated relative to each other, how they interact with each other, and how there are flows of electrical currents.

But that is all. It says nothing about concepts such as *love, hate, hope, fear, hunger, pain, joy or despair*. Open any physics book and these will not be mentioned. They are not part of the language of the physical sciences. There is no way they can get into scientific discourse. Why? Because these are concepts that belong to another way of speaking, another way of knowing, another approach to reality.

The reason why this limitation to science is so important is that when we talk of God, we specifically refer to a *personal* God – a God who is consciously aware of us, a God who knows us and loves us. We are talking of a Divine Mind.

That, of course, is not how some people use the word 'God'. When Hawking talks of 'knowing the mind of God', the phrase is simply a manner of speaking. The same goes for

Einstein. When expressing distaste for the unpredictable nature of quantum theory, he was moved to say, 'God does not play dice'. But he did not mean this to be taken literally. As far as can be gathered, Einstein, like Hawking today, did not believe in a personal God. The word 'God' in such expressions is simply another way of referring to 'nature'.

But for religious believers, as we have said, God is personal; he has a mind. So, when we ask whether God exists, what we are actually asking is whether behind nature there lies a supreme Mind. That being the case, the last place one should be seeking an answer is from science – a pursuit that does not even recognize the existence of human minds.

SAME DIFFERENCE

But is that really true? Is it really true that science has no truck with mind?

There are some who would claim that 'mind' is simply another name for 'brain'. Those who make exaggerated claims for science would certainly have us believe so.

And, in a way, they might well be right. We certainly know that there is some connection between what happens physically in the brain, and what concurrently happens psychologically in the mind. The swallowing of an aspirin (a physical occurrence) is accompanied by relief from a headache (a mental occurrence).

So, are brain and mind just one reality looked at in different ways? Or are they two distinct types of reality with some kind of link between them, such that what happens to one is reflected in what happens to the other?

We don't know, and there is no way of deciding. Why do I say that?

Remember what we said about science not explaining what

things *are*? This means it cannot say what the brain actually *is* – only how its various parts behave. It turns out that psychology is in the same boat: it talks about mental experiences, but can tell us nothing about the stuff out of which these mental experiences are made. Thus, at a deep fundamental level we are equally incapable of specifying the nature of brain processes and of mental experiences. That being the case, it is simply impossible to say for certain that they are the same – or alternatively, that they are distinct.

All we can be certain of is that, for a full description of what goes on, we do need to make use of *both ways of talking* – one in which we talk about physical happenings and one where we talk of mental experiences. As conscious human beings, we know that a description of ourselves purely in terms of chemical changes and electrical flows does not in any way capture the sense of what it is to be a thinking being. Science is powerless to say anything about the latter.

HUMANS, CYBORGS, WORMS AND BRICKS

The importance of this cannot be overstressed: There is absolutely no way that a purely scientific investigation of physical particles moving about in space and time under the influence of physical forces can yield the conclusion that one particular arrangement of matter (in the form of a human brain) is accompanied by mental experiences, whereas another (a TV set, say) is not.

Now, of course, it is perfectly true that from the time we were little more than a baby, each of us accepted that we were surrounded by human beings who had minds like ourselves. Indeed, one's very conception of oneself as a person is inescapably bound up with seeing oneself in relationship to other people.

And yet, if we set ourselves the task of *justifying* our normally unthinking acceptance of the existence of other people's minds, we find that it is uncommonly difficult. It certainly cannot be done in any watertight way.

For example, if I were to make the attempt, I must start from where I am: All I can be sure about – *absolutely* sure about – is that I myself have mental experiences. That is because they are given to me in direct experience.

I can't experience anyone else's mental experiences, so as far as anyone else's mind is concerned, I have to rely on indirect evidence. Which brings me basically to two ways of justifying a belief in other minds.

Firstly, other human beings *tell* me that they have conscious mental experiences. This isn't proof; they might be lying; they might be on a par with one of these new-fangled cyborgs one sees in science fiction movies these days – robots that look exactly like humans and are computer programmed to make all the right responses to any questions asked. But I reckon that's unlikely.

I think it particularly unlikely when other people not only tell me they are conscious but go on to provide useful information relevant to my own mental experiences. For example, they might warn me not to touch a kettle or I'll get scalded. When I foolishly ignore the warning and, sure enough, get hurt, it seems only reasonable to conclude that the original information came from a source that knew what it was talking about – it had experience of pain.

That, then, is the first reason for accepting that other humans have minds – the information I receive from them.

The second reason for accepting other minds is that I see bodies similar to my own. I know that, for whatever reason, there is a close connection between my physical body and my mental experiences. Bang my shin and I feel pain. So when I see your body, and note that by and large (give or take the odd wrinkle and difference in waistline) it looks like mine, it seems only reasonable to assume that it too will be accompanied by mental experiences. Bang its shin, and another mind will experience pain.

It is an argument by analogy. After all, why should my body be the only one that has an accompanying mind? The assumption that other bodies have minds I judge to be more *reasonable* than the only alternative: that for some unexplained reason, my body is unique in having a mind.

Now I can well imagine that by this stage you might be getting impatient. ('What *is* he on about? *Of course* other people have minds!!!')

All right. Let us get to more difficult cases – ones where the supposed other mind does not provide me with much, if any, information, and is accompanied by a body that is *not* an almost exact copy of my own.

Cats, dogs, horses and cows? Yes, I am happy to grant that these have minds.

Fish? Here we begin to move into a grey area. I personally would give them the benefit of the doubt. Some people (fishermen), however, prefer to think that a hook in the roof of the mouth causes no discomfort.

Worms? Now, that's an interesting one. When they are (inadvertently) sliced through by a spade, they writhe. Surely a sign of pain. But is it? Note how *both* halves are writhing. What does that mean? Are they *both* in pain? Does the worm now have *two* minds, whereas previously it had only one? Or does the worm have no mind at all? Looked at from the physical point of view one could account for the movements of the two halves of the body purely in terms of the flow of electrical currents and the chemical changes consequent on the physical act of severance. But then again, that is *always* the case; one can always offer a self-consistent account of what is happening purely in physical terms – including, as we saw, the case of human beings.

Then what about computers and artificial intelligence? Who has not wondered from time to time whether at some point in the future, as computers become more complex and powerful in their operations, they will eventually become conscious – they will feel pain, they will fall in love with each other, they will pray to God?

Again, there is no way of answering such a question with certainty. If I cannot be 100 per cent sure that *you* are conscious, how could I ever be sure about a computer? For the record, I will just say that if a computer's complexity were to rival that of the human brain, I would consider it only reasonable (again note that word) to accord it the benefit of the doubt.

WHO CARES?

If we can't prove the existence of these minds, does it matter what we believe about them?

A moment's reflection shows that it *does* matter. Whether we believe something has a mind or not governs how we treat that object. We think nothing of kicking a football; we do not go around kicking cats.

Our behaviour, the way we live our lives, is thus strongly affected by the *interpretation* we put on our physical observations. Though there is not a scrap of scientific data that can clinch the issue, we are driven again and again to make a decision as to whether or not to interpret our findings as suggestive of the existence of minds.

By now you may be wondering what the relevance of all this is. Simply this. When asking about the existence of God, what we are doing is enquiring as to whether there is a Mind behind, and through, *everything* – a Mind with whom we can enter into a personal relationship by whatever means, whether directly through prayer or, as in the case of human communications, through physical channels of communication acting as intermediaries.

God is to be found in the overall *interpretation* – the overall interpretation of *everything*. Does the sum total of all life's experience make better sense under the assumption that there is a Mind behind everything, or is it more reasonable to assume that there is no Mind? That is the question.

Because by the very nature of the problem there can be no incontrovertible proof of the existence of the Mind (as with mind in general), it is not surprising that people arrive at different interpretations.

The fact that there is no universally agreed answer to the question does not bother me. What does bother me is that there are many people who demand some kind of tangible proof of the existence of God's Mind, before taking him seriously. That seems to me to make as much sense as to treat your fellow human beings, and the animal kingdom, as not having minds because again there is not, and cannot be, that kind of evidence. Why demand of God a level and type of proof that is not regarded as necessary in other walks of life?

9 Now There's a Funny Thing

A MOST PECULIAR UNIVERSE

The Universe that emerged from the Big Bang was one that had a remarkable characteristic: it gave rise to life.

'Of course it did,' you might reply. 'We wouldn't be here if it hadn't!'

True. If there is someone around to ask questions about the world, then the world must obviously be of a type hospitable to life.

Yet there *is* something odd going on. After all, why should there be people around asking these questions? It is perfectly possible to imagine a universe without conscious inhabitants – one that exists, but no one is around to know that it does exist. In fact, such a universe ought to be the norm. A universe coming into existence kitted out with some *arbitrary* selection of physical laws, would have virtually zero chance of being suitable for the development of living creatures.

This is something that has only recently been recognized. It has caused a great stir, and is seen to be one of the biggest unsolved mysteries of our time. It goes under the name of 'the Anthropic Principle'.

The principle draws attention to a number of strange 'coincidences', each of which was necessary for life to develop.

Let's imagine that we are about to make a universe – one that is to lead to the development of life. To keep things simple we shall assume that it is a universe somewhat like ours, in that it starts with a Big Bang.

COINCIDENCE NUMBER 1

The first thing to be decided is how violent to make the explosion. Make it a little more violent than ours, and the matter is so quickly dispersed that it has no time for local condensations to form under the action of gravity to produce galaxies and stars. Make it a little less violent, and the stars and planets form all right, and evolution gets underway. But then disaster strikes. The gravitational attraction between the galaxies brings the slow expansion of the universe to a halt. From then on, all the matter of the universe collapses back together, we get a Big Crunch, and that's the end of that. If we are not careful, the universe will be all over and done with before the higher life-forms have had a chance to develop.

So, the conditions of the Big Bang have to be just right: not so violent as to disperse the matter too quickly; not so weak that the outwards motion of the galaxies cannot be sustained long enough to allow evolution to produce intelligent life-forms. The margin of error is very tight. And yet our actual Universe managed this delicate balancing act!

COINCIDENCE NUMBER 2

The next problem is how to get the raw materials for building the bodies of living creatures – particularly carbon. Carbon is an especially sticky kind of atom vital to the formation of the large complicated molecules of biological interest.

The difficulty is that no carbon comes out of the Big Bang. Why? We already saw in Chapter 1 that what comes out of a Big Bang depends on the conditions prevailing at the time. It has to be violent (to prevent everything collapsing back into a premature Big Crunch). That means there is very little time for the initial neutrons and protons to fuse to produce the nuclei of heavier atoms before the material disperses and the temperature drops. Essentially all that comes out of the Big Bang are the lightest gases: hydrogen, deuterium and helium.

Somehow we have to find a way of fusing these light nuclei together to form all the other types of atom we shall be needing later. Where can we do this? What we need is a nice hot oven.

Fortunately we do not have to look far: stars make ideal nuclear ovens. Excellent.

So, does that mean we are home and dry? I'm afraid not. The trouble is that to form carbon we have to arrange for three helium nuclei to fuse all about the same time. It's like having snooker balls bouncing around and hoping that three will all arrive at the same spot together. Collisions between *two* balls – no problem. But three? Decidedly tricky! So tricky, one could be forgiven for thinking that this would be a good point at which to give up our design study for a life-bearing universe.

Except that we notice the actual Universe *did* manage to negotiate this hurdle! But how?

Through something called a 'resonance'.

To get some idea of what a resonance is, we have only to think of a child on a swing. If the child pushes on the swing by moving its legs at random, it won't get very far. Some of the leg movements will be timed correctly to help get the swing going, but others will not; these will act against the motion of the swing and tend to slow it down again. But, once the child has been taught to swing its legs in time with the motion of the swing, the same effort produces a large effect. It is all a matter of carefully matching the pushes to the characteristics of the swing.

Now something of the same kind can occur when one nucleus collides with – or pushes on – another. If the conditions of the pushing (in this case the energies of the colliding particles) are just right, the resulting effect can be huge. The energies at which these resonances occur depend upon the values of certain physical constants (the numbers appearing in the equations governing the process).

By a quite extraordinary coincidence, one of these nuclear resonances occurs exactly at the energy needed to allow three helium nuclei to collide to produce carbon. Thus an effect which should have been tiny becomes – against all the odds – spectacularly large. In this way we get our carbon.

And, I suppose one ought to add, having got the carbon with the help of the resonance, there are fortunately no further resonances around to convert all the carbon into oxygen. A little oxygen will be needed later, but we do not want all the carbon converting.

COINCIDENCE NUMBER 3

Which brings us to the next hurdle: that of *location*. We have our carbon all right, but *where* is it? It's in the middle of a star – at a temperature of millions of degrees. A fat lot of good that is!

There's nothing for it, we have to find a way of getting the carbon out. But how? We know how difficult it is trying to get something up into space from the surface of the Earth; it takes a powerful rocket. The gravitational pull of a star is vastly more than that of the Earth – and there are no rockets to call on. Yet another invitation to abandon our design study?

No. There *must* be a way of doing it; the actual Universe clearly succeeded somehow. So let's think; what happens to a star eventually?

Throughout its life it radiates energy. This is the energy generated in its nuclear processes. The interior has to be hot, otherwise the star would collapse in on itself. The strong inward gravitational force has to be balanced, and this is done by having the particles in the interior furiously rushing about, banging into each other and generally keeping their neighbours at a distance.

But there comes a time, as the star gets old, when it comes to the end of its fuel. It is still merrily radiating energy away, but without compensating for the loss. Like someone spending more than they are earning, this is a situation that cannot go on. The interior starts to cool; the particles become less energetic in their movements. As a result, they are less able to withstand gravity, so they get packed down more tightly. Because they are now closer to each other, the particles exert even stronger gravitational forces on each other. This leads to further contraction. This in turn leads to yet stronger gravity . . . more contraction . . . and so on.

A point is reached where everything suddenly goes completely out of control. The star can no longer hold itself up; it undergoes catastrophic collapse. This causes an almighty explosion. It is one of the most remarkable occurrences in the Universe. Talk about going out with a bang! It is called a 'supernova'. The last one to hit the headlines was in 1987 – you might recall the excitement at the time.

It is the blast of the supernova explosion that drives out some of the material of the star – including the newly fused nuclei of carbon, oxygen etc.

But hold on. That's a bit odd, isn't it? An *im*plosion that gives rise to an *ex*plosion. Yes, it is odd. In fact, it took physicists a long time to understand how that could possibly be. But we now think we know the answer. It is a burst of neutrinos that blasts the material out.

The mechanism was not obvious. We are used to the idea that neutrinos hardly ever interact with anything. (Recall how it was the unnoticed neutrino emitted from the radioactive decay that gave the appearance of energy not being conserved.) Neutrinos are very slippery customers. Those coming from the Sun, for example, can pass right through the Earth a million times before they have a decent chance of hitting anything. And yet it is the neutrinos that allow the carbon to do its Houdini act of escaping from the star.

So, thanks to supernovae, the Universe has this cunning way of getting the recycled material thrown out into space.

What happens to it then? It re-collects to form new stars. One of these was the Sun. These stars, unlike the first-generation stars, could have planets. Planets could not form first time round because the dirt needed had first to be manufactured from the original hydrogen and helium – and that, as we now know, was done in the first generation of stars.

One of the planets was Earth. Benefitting from a particularly favourable climate, evolution was able to get under way on this planet, and presumably on many, many other planets going round stars elsewhere in the Universe. From inanimate chemicals, primitive life-forms began to appear – so primitive it would be hard to know whether they were properly to be classified as 'living' or not – somewhat like modern-day viruses. Then, through the process of evolution by natural selection, more complicated forms of life appeared – forms with sufficiently intricate brains that the creatures became conscious. And so on to human beings. This process of evolution took 4,500 million years.

COINCIDENCE NUMBER 4

Yes, that's right: 4,500 million years. It's a long time. During all that time a steady source of energy was required to keep things moving along – the energy supplied by the Sun. Which brings us to yet another problem: What is the Sun? It's a nuclear bomb! It's a nuclear bomb going off *slowly* – over the desired period of thousands of millions of years.

Here on Earth, scientists have spent forty years and hundreds of millions of pounds trying to build machines capable of letting off a hydrogen bomb slowly so that we can harness nuclear fusion power for peaceful purposes. Considerable progress has been made, but it is still reckoned that there are another fifty years to go before it becomes a commercial proposition.

The Sun manages it without any help! To bring this about requires the most delicate balance between, on the one hand, the gravitational constant responsible for determining how much matter collects together to form the Sun – in other words how much fuel the fire has to draw on – and on the other hand, the constant determining the strength of the nuclear forces and how fast the nuclear reactions proceed. Yet another strange coincidence.

In fact, we are lucky to have any stars at all. To get a star to burn, the gravitational force has to be such that the right amount of matter condenses to raise the temperature to the kinds of value needed for reactions based on some entirely different force – the nuclear force – to be triggered. It need not have been that way. There are stars called 'brown dwarfs'. They are not proper stars; they did not quite make it. They collected a lot of matter together, it heated up as it condensed; but not sufficiently to trigger the nuclear processes – so they fizzled out. It is easy to imagine a world in which the force of gravity was weaker than ours, to the extent that no collection of matter was sufficient to ensure that the star caught fire.

AND SO ON...

We have spoken only about the coincidences that seemed to have conspired together to produce the right physical conditions for the development of life – coincidences that are collectively referred to as the Anthropic Principle.

One could doubtless add many more coincidences, of a biological type, that marked the evolutionary progress of life from its primitive beginnings to its culmination in humankind. There are, after all, a number of stages along the way where it is very difficult to envisage how evolving life-forms managed to bridge the gap to the next higher stage. Let me hasten to add, however, that none should be regarded as sufficiently serious as to justify our abandoning the idea that we evolved ultimately from inanimate chemicals. Nevertheless, there may well be some pretty improbable coincidences of a biological nature to add to the already formidable catalogue that arises from physics.

Exactly how unlikely is it that the coincidences that make up the Anthropic Principle happened purely by chance? It is hard, if not impossible, to put a number on it. One can say, for example, that the gravitational constant (the number that governs the strength of the gravitational force) would need to lie within a certain range for life to have had a chance of developing. But what are we to compare that range to? How extreme a value could we imagine the constant having? From zero to infinity? If that were the case, the chances of the actual value falling within our desired limited range would be zero.

The same difficulty is encountered with the other features

we have discussed. In each case, it is hard to quote a figure for the odds; all we *can* say is that the overall odds against getting a physical world such as ours are absolutely immense – much greater than those against winning the football pools.

So, what *are* we to make of it all?

10 He Who Fixed It

A COSMIC ARCHITECT?

For religious believers, the Anthropic Principle poses no problem. The cosmos is the way it is because that is how God designed it. He designed it specifically for the creation of life – to bring into being creatures who could relate to him. The so-called 'coincidences' of the last chapter are *not* coincidences at all. God deliberately arranged them to be that way.

By that, one does not mean he designed the world just for human beings. When one surveys the cosmos – the immense number of stars, many possessing planets – one must surely conclude that there is extraterrestrial life, and that some of this life will be as intelligent as ourselves, if not more so. God will be every bit as interested in and concerned about them as ourselves.

Mind you, we have to admit that it's an odd kind of 'home' for living creatures. Steven Weinberg, in the Epilogue to *The First Three Minutes* from which we have already quoted, speaks of 'an overwhelmingly hostile universe'. He has a point. The astronauts confronting the bleak wastes of the Moon were moved to speak warmly of the friendly-looking Earth above their heads. And the more one has learned of the conditions on the Sun's other planets, the more we have come to appreciate those that prevail here on planet Earth. As for the stars, clearly there is no place there for living creatures.

Yes, Weinberg is right inasmuch as most locations in the Universe are hostile to life. And yet, can we *really* regard the Universe as hostile – life as nothing more than a 'farcical' by-product – when we consider how things *might* have been? Bearing in mind the fantastic odds against there being *anywhere* in a universe that could support life, it could be argued that the Designer of this world has bent over backwards to make it user-friendly!

WORLDS WITHOUT END

Is there an alternative to accepting God as the Designer of the cosmos?

Yes. An infinite number of universes. That's right. There is a serious suggestion, made by certain scientists, that in addition to our Universe, there are a vast number of other universes, each of them operating according to its own laws.

The vast, vast majority of these universes are not hospitable to the development of life. In the occasional freak universe, one has, purely by chance, a set of laws that do give rise to the right conditions. As living creatures we have to inhabit one of the freak universes.

This way there are no real coincidences; the chance of any particular universe supporting life is poor, but there are so many attempts, a handful of them must succeed.

In this connection, it has to be said that although this idea of an infinite number of universes has been put forward by scientists, it is not itself to be regarded as a scientific theory.

In the first place it cannot be checked out. Other universes are not part of our experience. 'Another universe' specifically

refers to a world that we cannot contact. Thus, we can never be sure that it exists, let alone find out what it might be like. It must remain the object of speculation – and speculation is not science.

In the second place, one of the features of the scientific endeavour is that one continually strives for simplicity – fewer basic constituents, fewer forces, fewer laws – this is what we noted earlier. It is the application of what we call Occam's Razor. Now one can hardly imagine anything *less* in accord with Occam's Razor than a postulate of an infinite number of universes all run according to different laws!

No, this suggestion is not science. But that in itself is no reason to dismiss it out of hand. If people prefer to interpret the cosmos that way, rather than accept a Designer God, then that has to be their choice.

AN ARGUMENT FROM DESIGN

As far as I am concerned, there is little doubt that where the Anthropic Principle is concerned, believers are in pole position. So much so that there is the temptation to use the Anthropic Principle as a knock-down argument for God's existence – a stick with which to beat the unbelievers: 'You simply *must* believe in God; the alternative is just too ridiculous for words.'

Many years ago, the eminent cosmologist, Fred Hoyle, caused something of a furore. He delivered a series of Reith Lectures on the BBC in which he made some militantly atheistic remarks. These days, without actually using the word 'God', he speaks freely of 'He who fixed it'. Why?

It was Hoyle who first suggested that carbon might be synthesized in stars through a resonance. Though the improbability of such a resonance seemed overwhelming, he could see no alternative. Soon afterwards, his brilliant conjecture was proved correct.

The episode appears to have left its mark on Hoyle. The sheer unlikeliness of it all seems to have given his atheism something of a jolt.

Should we perhaps take our cue from this, and use the Anthropic Principle to jolt other people's atheism?

A CAUTIONARY TALE

Careful! We have already had experience of what can happen when one goes down that kind of path.

There was an earlier argument for God's existence based on the idea of design – the design of our bodies and those of other living creatures:

On considering the intricacy of the human body – the wonderful way all its limbs and organs fulfil their functions – it is hard to escape the conclusion that it has been purpose-built. Just as the discovery of a watch on a beach points to the existence of the unseen watchmaker, so the mechanism of the human body points to the unseen divine hand that fashioned it. Such was the argument.

The rug was pulled from underneath it a long time ago by Darwin's Theory of Evolution by Natural Selection.

According to this theory, animals that happen by chance to be born with some characteristic giving them the edge over their rivals, are the ones more likely to succeed in the struggle to survive. They have the better chance of reaching the stage where they can mate. They are therefore more likely to pass on their beneficial characteristic to their offspring, than their rivals are to pass on the less beneficial ones. The result is that the next generation is, on average, better suited for survival than the preceding one.

The process is then all set to repeat itself. Over many, many generations, the progressive accumulation of beneficial characteristics can give the impression that the animal has been custom-designed for the kind of life it leads.

But this is illusory. The 'good design' has come about purely through random changes. It did not require a designer; the watch did not need a watchmaker.

A reminder of the demise of the old Argument from Design is to be found today in the title of Richard Dawkins' well-known book, *The Blind Watchmaker*.

What had to be learned from this episode was the fact that it was misguided to try and use the idea of design as a knock-down argument to wield against unbelievers.

So, there we have it: we have learned our lesson. Except...

Except that we are now presented with what seems to be

the father-and-mother of an Argument from Design! Not a biological argument based on the 'design' of the human body this time, but a physical argument based on the 'design' of the cosmos.

Is that our cue to go into battle again? I would urge caution. Why? Quite simply because we might well discover one of these days that all these extraordinary features of the cosmos – all these coincidences – are not actually extraordinary or coincidental at all; there might be some perfectly rational explanation for them.

Already, with a variant of the Big Bang theory called the Inflationary Theory, we seem to have a reason why it is unlikely the Universe could ever have undergone premature recollapse (thereby coming to an end in a Big Crunch before evolution had played its part).

According to this idea, the Universe underwent a particularly rapid period of expansion – called 'inflation' – at a very early stage. When this period ended, it left the Universe in a finely tuned state, such that the type of expansion it is now undergoing is destined eventually to come to a halt – but only just. The halting of the galaxies, and the onset of recollapse, will occur only at some time in the infinite future.

That doesn't get rid of the first coincidence. We are still left with the problem of how come there was this mechanism in place for so fine-tuning the expansion. But there is no doubt that the inflationary idea does begin to hint at the possibility that one day we might be able to explain away the first 'coincidence' based on the rate of expansion.

It might well be that the other features described earlier will similarly fall into place one day. That is why I think it best to go easy on how one uses the Anthropic Principle. I suspect the overzealous might again end up with egg on their face.

IF YOU CAN'T BEAT 'EM, JOIN 'EM

And if all the coincidences *are* one day accounted for in a natural way, as happened over the old Argument from Design, what then?

That would not mean that God's hand could not still be seen at work. After all, look what happened over the old argument concerning the 'design' of humans. We now see evolution as God's special way of bringing humans into existence. In a sense he did design us; it's just that he used a natural process to do it. It is a process that itself reveals something of his own divine nature: his inexhaustible patience; his willingness to bide his time when it comes to accomplishing his ends.

And just consider what light it throws on human nature to think of humans as products of evolution by natural selection. It means that just as other animals have built-in instincts, we are also likely to have them. And those genetically acquired behaviour traits are those that, by and large, are selfish and self-seeking – aimed at the survival of the self, or of one's own kin.

But this surely is just a different way of looking at something that religious believers have long known about – original sin – a tendency from conception to be selfcentred, seeking to do one's own will, rather than that of God.

No, there's no doubt in my mind that if one is willing to embrace the findings of modern science, there are rich spiritual insights to be gained. And what happened over evolution and human design can happen again over the Anthropic Principle. I am confident that if the so-called coincidences that make up that principle also one day receive scientific explanations, these explanations will themselves be further sources of enlightenment about the ways of God, and should be welcomed as such.

11 God in the Crevices?

AN INVITATION TO THE LION'S DEN

I have warned against the idea of trying to use the overall design of the Universe as a would-be 'proof' of God's existence. Indeed, I believe *any* attempt to provide watertight evidence for God's existence – evidence that would convince a sceptic – is doomed to failure. Yet time and again people make such demands of me. I suppose one has to put it down to the lingering influence of the Verification Principle, as I mentioned in Chapter 7.

I came across a classic example of this two or three months ago. I had been asked to give a talk at Imperial College in London. It was to be one of a series called the Blackett Lectures, so named after a former head of the Physics Department there. The lectures are open to anyone – staff or students.

For years they had been moribund; hardly anyone attended. But then a new person took over responsibilty for running them. He had a brilliant – if obvious – idea. He asked the students what they would *like* to hear about.

As you might expect at a college that concentrates on science and technology, the students wanted to hear about nuclear fusion, lasers, holograms etc. But they also expressed interest in having a talk about religious belief in a scientific age. That was how I came to be invited.

On arriving at the college, I was warned that certain members of staff had expressed hostility to the very idea of the Blackett Lectures being used for a talk involving religion. Some of them were likely to be present.

The lecture theatre was packed; all 250 seats were taken. In addition, students were sitting on the steps down both aisles, and stood crowded around the two rear doors. (I hasten to add, this was not because they had come to hear *me*! I doubt whether more than a handful would have known me from Adam. No, it was the subject that had drawn them.)

After I finished my prepared talk, the attack began – from the members of staff I had been told about. Talk about Daniel in the lion's den!

One of them poured scorn on 'this hypothetical Jesus of yours'. To which I replied, 'One of these days you'll discover just how hypothetical he is!'

It was all good knock-about stuff. Fun for spectators; but hardly constructive and helpful. I hated it. I never relish such occasions. I sometimes wonder why I allow myself to get involved in them.

GO ON – PROVE IT!

At one point in the discussion, one of the senior staff stood up and declared, 'But you have dodged the issue. You have not proved to my satisfaction that there is a God at all.'

Here was an academic – a highly educated man – who was labouring under the impression that my aim had been to *argue* him into believing in God. He honestly thought that it was reasonable for him to start out from a position of total scepticism, and be forced, against his wishes if necessary, into a belief.

It is a common misunderstanding. It was exactly the same

kind of attitude that Dr Richard Dawkins had shown at the science/religion debate I mentioned in the Introduction – the debate held in Edinburgh. There he had painted a picture of religious believers seeking 'evidence for God in the crevices between scientific explanations'.

In effect, what such people are claiming is that there is no need for them to take God's existence seriously, unless and until someone is able to pick up a science book and point out some phenomenon that scientists cannot explain – a feature of the way the world works that can only be accounted for by God's direct intervention.

But such a demand is quite unrealistic. It is a caricature of religious belief. I don't know of anyone who came to know God that way.

A GOD OF THE GAPS

How did such an idea arise? Doubtless because certain well-intentioned – though misguided – believers have in the past adopted just such a tactic in an attempt to convince the sceptical.

Thus it used to be claimed that thunder and lightning were direct manifestations of God's wrath. This was in the days before it was realized that such occurrences could be explained simply in terms of electricity. And there were many other examples of such arguments.

Together they added up to a 'God of the gaps' – a God who was to be found in the gaps between scientific knowledge.

It was a hopelessly mistaken way of arguing. It gave the impression of a God who had made a right mess of designing the world. The laws of nature he had devised couldn't cope properly; he had personally to keep intervening to plug the gaps.

Besides, there was the worrying feature that with each new advance of science, there were progressively less gaps to be plugged. Each fresh territory won for science was another lost to God. God was being relegated into playing a marginal, ever-diminishing role in the world.

Essentially the Argument from Design was just another example of this God-of-the-gaps approach: 'Scientists cannot explain how the human body came to be the way it is, therefore it must be God who did the designing.'

A similar type of argument based on the Anthropic Principle would seem to me to be no better.

NOT BY ARGUMENT ALONE

This is not to say that arguments have no part to play in bringing people to God. (I wouldn't be writing this book if I thought arguments were useless.)

They are particularly relevant for those genuinely willing to give religion a try – if only it can be shown that this can be done with intellectual integrity. For such people a vital first step to religious belief might be to hear arguments to the effect that there is no incompatibility between science and religion.

Arguments delivered in that spirit are fine, provided that it is recognized that arguments *alone* cannot get to the heart of faith. There has to come a point where one willingly surrenders oneself to an active, responsive, loving, accepting, relationship with God. God has to be known *personally*, through experiencing him directly.

This is done primarily through one's private prayer life. Additionally, one must be sensitive to the ways in which God makes himself known through other people – holy people – especially for Christians, through Jesus. He reveals himself through holy writings, and through the interpretation of history.

He is also to be found in the interpretation of the physical world. Note the word: *interpretation*. The interpretation of the whole cosmos – what it all adds up to. I am *not* talking about the explanation of any isolated piece of data.

MEANWHILE, BACK AT THE DEN

In that highly charged atmosphere of the college lecture theatre, I tried to explain all this to the academic who had challenged me that I had 'dodged the issue' in not proving there was a God.

But I don't think I made any headway with him. He was like the man who meticulously examines, one by one, every house, shop, factory, recreation ground and street – all in search of something labelled 'town planning'. He does not find it. Why? Is there no such thing as town planning? Of course there is. It's just that one does not discover it that way. Town planning can only be discerned by looking at the whole. Even then, it must be interpreted.

Let me not leave you with the impression that the Imperial College event was all unrelieved aggro. It wasn't. After twenty minutes discussion, there was the customary word of thanks from the chairman and a round of applause from the audience. That was that, I thought.

But no. While some departed for the exits, a crowd of students surged to the front to continue the discussion. Sitting perched on the edge of the bench, I did my best to answer their questions. In place of the clever, point-scoring debating that had gone on previously, we became deeply engaged over the next 1 hour 20 minutes exploring the issues in an earnest, constructive, sympathetic exchange of ideas.

Towards the end, a girl took me on one side and quietly thanked me for what I had said, and 'particularly for being brave enough to come here and stand up to the likes of *them*', she said, nodding in the direction of where the staff had been sitting. It's in such fleeting moments that I do understand why I get mixed up in all this.

12 Don't Touch!

THE GOD WHO RETIRED TO THE PAVILION

If God was clever enough to come up with a set of physical laws that could look after the normal day-to-day running of the place, without him having to be constantly plugging the gaps, does that mean he never gets a look in? All right, he saw to the Big Bang. But that only took an instant. After that, was there nothing more for him to do – other than generally keep the whole show in existence through his being the Sustainer of everything?

> With the success of scientific theories in describing events, most people have come to believe that God allows the Universe to evolve according to a set of laws and does not intervene in the Universe to break these laws.

In saying this in *A Brief History of Time*, Stephen Hawking is probably right. Most people do think that. They regard God as the divine groundsman who prepares the cricket pitch, marks it out, cuts the grass and erects the stumps. But then, having done his bit, he retires to the Heavenly pavilion to read his newspaper for the duration of the match.

But is this how it really is? Does God *never* intervene? Does he *never* make his presence directly felt by suspending the normal operation of the laws of nature – on special occasions, perhaps?

Though most people might not believe in miracles, they certainly expect bishops and clergy to believe in them. Hence the annual pilgrimage to Durham at Easter time – newspaper and TV reporters hoping for a sound-bite from Bishop David Jenkins about his not believing that the tomb of Jesus was empty. Anything for a headline: 'Bish Says Bosh to Resurrection!'

I also, as a preacher, am often asked, 'Do you believe in miracles?'

If I have to give a straight answer, then it has to be 'Yes.' But before you take that as your cue to skip to the next chapter, there are a number of caveats I would like to add. Indeed, having read the caveats, you might well end up thinking I should have answered 'No'!

BREAKING THE LAW

First we must be sure we know how we are using the word 'miracle'.

Strictly speaking, a miracle is any event that shows the presence of God in an especially vivid way. For example, there might be a terrible road crash – but everyone walks away from the scene unharmed. One of those involved might regard this as purely due to luck. Another, a religious believer, will give credit to God for his protection. The latter might freely speak of 'a miraculous escape' – without *necessarily* claiming that the laws of nature were temporarily suspended. In speaking of a miracle in this sense, one is going no further than acknowledging that, with the eye of faith, one sees here a particularly remarkable example of God's providence.

Can we accept miracles in this sense? Clearly there is no problem.

That, however, is not the point at issue. When people ask me about miracles, they have a narrower definition in mind. For them, a miracle is specifically a violation of a law of nature – God interrupting the smooth flow of nature. That's the definition we shall now stick to.

The second point to get clear is what we mean by a law of nature.

We have already seen that behind the bewildering array of phenomena that confront us, there are a few general rules of behaviour at work. It is an experimental observation that events appear to obey these rules or laws.

Does that mean that the laws are such that *every* event *must* conform to them?

One certainly cannot experimentally test every conceivable event. It has to be an article of *belief* that the laws *always* apply. (We had echoes of this earlier when we saw that the laws of nature are more open to falsification than verification.)

So scientists can never *prove* that miracles are impossible. All they can say is that, based on their long experience of the regular working of nature, if miracles do occur at all, their frequency is not as great as one might otherwise suppose – from a reading of the Bible, say.

WHOSE LAWS ARE THEY, ANYWAY?

But even though scientists can't actually demonstrate that miracles do not happen, could it not be argued that it is simply *impossible* for physical laws to be broken? Could it not be the case that even God would be *incapable* of performing miracles?

I see no reason why. God, as Creator and Sustainer, was the one who originally set up the laws, and continues to govern their day-to-day operation. They are *his* laws. As far as I'm concerned, he is free to do whatever he likes with them. I have no doubt that he can perform miracles, if he so wishes.

WILL HE, WON'T HE?

The question then becomes: Does he so wish?

Some people take the Bible at face value, and simply accept all the miracles as described. There is nothing to demonstrate that they are wrong in this. At this distance in time, there is no way of checking the stories out.

But there is certainly no *need* to accept all the miracle stories – not all of them lock, stock and barrel. This is what most biblical scholars say, and that has come to be my own position.

In the first place, some so-called miracles can be covered by the normal laws of nature; they are not miraculous in the narrow sense in which we are defining the word 'miracle'.

Take Moses feeding the Israelites on manna in the desert, for example. Manna is a syrupy secretion given out by insects called *trabutina mannipara*. It forms in sugary drops the size of peas. They harden on the leaves of tamarisk plants overnight, and then fall to the ground in the morning. Bedouin Arabs use manna as part of their normal diet between the months of May and July.

Similarly with the casting out of devils. Today these would not be accounted miraculous. Rather, they would be regarded as the work of a good psychiatrist.

Quite apart from 'miracles' that were not really miraculous, one or two miracle stories appear to have been generated by mistake. For instance, compare the following two stories:

(i) The disciples are in a boat on the Sea of Galilee. They see

Jesus walking on the water. Impetuous Peter gets out of the boat to go to him, and ends up in the water.

(ii) The disciples are in a boat on the Sea of Galilee. They see Jesus walking on the seashore (soon after the Resurrection). Impetuous Peter gets out of the boat to go to him and ends up swimming in the water.

They seem to be one and the same story – apart from Jesus in one account walking on the sea, and in the other, walking on the seashore.

Biblical scholars say that when one goes back to the original Greek, one finds an ambiguity between the phrase 'walking *on* the sea' and 'walking *by* the sea'. It seems pretty likely, therefore, that in the telling and retelling of this story, somewhere along the line someone got hold of the wrong end of the stick. Through a mistranslation, they unwittingly created a miracle story.

Personally I found it a relief to come across this suggestion as to how this particular story might have originated. I had never been able to understand why Jesus would have refused point blank to be tempted into defying gravity by throwing himself off a high building, but then went ahead and defied gravity by walking on water.

However, when all is said and done, few miracle stories can be disposed of either as naturalistic occurences, or as mistakes in translation. What about the others?

TALES OF WONDER

We need a background against which to view these stories. What we have to realize is that ancient people took a positive delight in tales of wondrous happenings. They had little or no interest in scientific questions – whether or not the incident described did actually happen.

This is amply demonstrated in some of the writings originally considered for inclusion in the Bible, but ultimately rejected. These books were particularly rampant with extraordinary stories.

For example, an account of Jesus as a boy making clay models of birds that promptly flew out of the window; Jesus being placed as an infant on a mule's back, which then miraculously turned into a young man; Jesus cursing his school teacher who promptly fell down dead; etc.

Blatant invention. No wonder they were excluded! But the existence of such writings does create a niggling doubt: Can we be sure that *none* of that sort of invention was going on in the books that *did* get accepted as scripture?

To answer that we look at stories that are dealt with by more than one gospel. We compare the earlier version with the later one.

Take, for example, the arrest of Jesus. In Mark, the first of the gospels to be written, we see how one of Jesus' followers cut off the ear of the high priest's servant. That's all that happens: the ear is simply cut off. By the time we get to the later writing of Luke, Jesus performs a miracle: he puts the ear back on and heals it. If this truly happened, it is incomprehensible why Mark, in telling the same story, omits to mention the extraordinary miracle. The only sensible conclusion appears to be that, between the writing of the two gospels, some invention has been going on.

Further evidence for the proliferation of miracle stories with time comes when we place the epistles and gospels in chronological order.

Paul's epistles are the earliest writings. Apart from the Resurrection, he mentions none of Jesus' miracles. By the time we get to Mark, we read of the stilling of the waters, the raising of Jairus' daughter, the feeding of the multitude, the walking on water, and various healing miracles. Most of these are to be found in Matthew and Luke (who used Mark as a source), but in addition there are others, among them the Virgin Birth, and the ear of the high priest's servant being healed. Lastly we have John, who introduces yet more miracles – turning water into wine, the healing of the man born blind, etc.

We cannot be certain, but it does seem that more and more of these stories came into circulation as time progressed.

HOODWINKING, OR SOMETHING ELSE?

What is going on? Does this all add up to an attempt to deceive us? We can only answer that if we get to grips with the true nature of a miracle story.

In Chapter 2 we saw how the Jews lived in a story-telling culture. They passed on the fruits of their wisdom in stories such as the Genesis creation accounts. What mattered were the deep spiritual messages they contained – messages that were to be relevant to future generations when they in their turn had to face the same fundamental problems and questions concerning the meaning of life. It was this same story-telling tradition that was later to be carried on by Jesus in the form of his parables.

Could it be that some at least of the miracle stories were originated in the same spirit?

Certainly many of the biblical miracles have a lot to teach us today. Time and again they illustrate in vivid, concrete form some underlying deep spiritual truth.

To see what these inner truths might be, it is best to turn to John. He was writing primarily for non-Jewish readers –

people who perhaps were not in tune with Jewish customs and ways of thought, and had to have the underlying spiritual messages spelt out for them. Let us look at some miracles as they are told in John:

(i)   *The feeding of the multitude.* It is an occasion on which Jesus describes *himself* as the Bread of Life. Although he is feeding people physically, what he is directing their attention to is spiritual hunger.

(ii) *The raising of Lazarus.* Jesus says on this occasion that he is the Resurrection and the Life. Note: he *is* – not he will be. Thus eternal life is something we participate in now; it is not something we have to look forward to – which is what Martha had earlier replied when asked a question on the subject.

(iii) *The cure of the man born blind.* Jesus says here that he is the Light of the World. The thrust of the incident is the truth about spiritual blindness.

(iv) *The Virgin Birth.* Jesus' uniqueness as both God and man is what this story is all about – the joining together of divinity and humanity into a seamless union. What more graphic imagery could there be to illuminate this rather abstract truth than an account of a virgin being over-lain by the Holy Spirit?

So there is no doubt about the spiritual content of biblical miracle stories. But this still leaves open the question of whether these spiritually deep stories also refer to actual physical events that happened as described.

At this distance we cannot tell. To some extent it is pointless arguing about them. I would rather ask, 'Does it *matter* whether they happened?'

Here I think the answer is 'No.' It is surely a weak and inadequate relationship with God that clings to miracles to bolster faith. As Jesus once said: 'It is an evil and adulterous generation that seeks for a sign'.

Given that one's faith is firmly grounded elsewhere, it matters not whether the miracles happened – provided that the underlying spiritual truths are taken to heart.

BUT WHAT ABOUT THE BISHOP?

I brought up the subject of the Bishop of Durham, so I'd better tell you what I think about him and his views.

The spiritual truth behind the story of the empty tomb on the first Easter Day is that Jesus has conquered death, that he is alive, that he is with me as I write these words; he is with you as you read them. He is someone who knows our innermost thoughts now, and can communicate with us through prayer. His presence is as real as yours or mine.

Anyone who believes that, believes in the Resurrection; they can count themselves a fully paid-up, *bona fide* Christian. David Jenkins, as I understand from reports about his beliefs, satisfies those conditions.

Whether, in addition, one accepts that the tomb was physically empty 2,000 years ago is, so I believe, neither here nor there. For the record, I happen to believe that it was empty. I happen to believe that probably quite a number of the miracles – particularly those of healing – also occurred as described.

In other words, the God I believe in is not like the cricket groundsman who retires for the duration of the match. He is more like a *real* groundsman – the kind of groundsman I used to work under when, as a cricket-crazy youth, I was on the ground staff at the Kennington Oval Ground. During the match, Bert Lock was always around, always alert. At the slightest hint of rain he would have his lads ready to rush out with the covers as soon as called upon. As the innings drew to a close, he'd be ready with the broom, the white paint brush and the roller – all set to make good the pitch. And at all times he kept his beady eye on my performance as I worked the main score-box. Yes, Bert was always there, always poised to intervene and help out when called upon.

THE IRON FIST IN THE VELVET GLOVE

Finally, let us suppose, contrary to the belief I have just expressed, that God *never* intervenes in a miraculous way. What would that imply about God's relationship with the world? Would that mean that having got the world going at the Big Bang, it was then a case of hands off?

Not at all. To understand why, I find it helpful to think of God in relation to the physical world in much the same way as we conscious beings are in relation to our physical bodies.

In Chapter 8 we were discussing the relationship between the brain and the mind. We saw there a correlation between the physical events going on in the brain – the flows of electricity and the chemical changes – and the psychological experiences of the mind.

But exactly what kind of relationship is it? Suppose for the sake of argument, you were to feel that you had done enough reading for today. You decide to close the book and go and make yourself a cup of coffee. Corresponding to this mental decision to do something different, what happens in your brain?

One viewpoint holds that if a scientist were closely examining the contents of your brain at the time, he would observe something odd. First there would be all the processes accompanying your mental state of reading this book and growing tired and bored. Suddenly, without warning, all that changes. What happens next is the establishment of a new pattern – one that corresponds to you closing the book and rising out of your seat.

How did the one pattern of behaviour get transformed into the other? According to the view we are considering, physics is powerless to say. An entirely new and unpredictable influence came into operation. It momentarily interrupted the normal working of the physical laws – causing, in effect, a minor miracle. In this way, the mental decision to do something different exerts a direct influence on the brain.

This is how some people believe we, as conscious human beings exercise our free will. We make mental decisions and, depending on our choice of action, the course of physical nature is altered. First it is altered in our brain, and then, through the brain sending signals to our muscles, elsewhere through our resulting actions.

Those who subscribe to this view of how the mental relates to the physical should have no difficulty accepting miracles. In much the same way as our own mind can influence what happens within the confines of the brain, God's Mind, lying behind the whole physical world, would be able to intervene at will anywhere.

But this is *not* the majority view of scientists as to what is likely to be going on in the brain. This brings us to the second possibility.

Processes in the brain are just as much subject to the laws of nature as physical processes anywhere else. A scientist examining your brain as you make your decision to stop reading the book would observe *nothing* odd. Those processes corresponding to your reading and getting bored would be found to develop in a perfectly natural way into those involving you shutting the book, getting up, and going off to make the coffee.

If this really is the situation, does that put paid to free will? When you 'decided' to stop reading, did you actually make a decision at all – or would you have stopped reading at that point anyway?

It's a worrying thought. After all, a scientist examining your brain could presumably have worked out from what was happening earlier, what decision you were due to make and when you were going to make it (assuming there had been sufficient past experience of this kind of investigation to be able to recognize which particular brain processes accompany which mental decisions). Your decision would be known to the investigating scientist even before it was known to you.

The curious thing is that free will does *not* thereby get discarded. Granted, the scientist might say afterwards that, from his vantage-point – from the observations he made on your brain – he had known what you were going to decide before you knew. But from *your* vantage-point – that of someone having to live out one's life – the exercise of the will remains indispensible. It makes absolutely no sense for you to sit there reading this book and saying, 'I don't have to make up my mind when to stop reading; when the working out of the laws of nature in my brain dictates that I shall stop, then I shall stop.'

Life simply isn't like that. Without a positive decision to make a cup of coffee, you won't get one.

The notion that we freely make decisions, which we then act upon, is absolutely inescapable; it is central to the description of the conscious life. What the scientist sees happening in the brain has, therefore, to be open to the interpretation that it is the physical correlate of a free-will decision. That interpretation of what goes on has to have at least the same weight as the alternative, which is to regard the mental act as the correlate of physical events following their natural course.

How these two interpretations are to live side by side, nobody really understands. For centuries, the problem has refused to yield up a satisfying solution. I suspect that is how it always will be – one of life's deep mysteries.

It is the same mystery that lies at the heart of how God, the Supreme Mind, makes decisions that are reflected in what goes on in the physical world. If we can't fully grasp the relationship between our own decisions and their effect on the world, can we *really* expect to understand how God's decisions come to manifest themselves physically?

What we *can* say is that, even if God does not intervene miraculously, that does not make him an absentee landlord – any more than we, as conscious beings, would be rendered irrelevant if it were to be discovered one day that the physical processes in our brains do indeed always obey the laws of nature.

Just as the very working out of the laws in a human brain would continue to match and reveal the mental experiences of that person, so the working out of the laws throughout the entire cosmos would match and reveal the Divine Mind behind all things.

It was the same when I worked at the Oval. Quite apart from Bert's obvious interventions in the proceedings during the match, there was another way his influence was at work – an all-pervasive influence:

An experienced groundsman can produce any kind of pitch: fast or slow; one on which the ball rears like a bucking bronco, others where it keeps low; pitches that remain a batsman's paradise to the last ball, others where they start to break up and take deadly spin from the second day.

It's all a matter of preparation – how the pitch is watered, how it is fed with fertilizer and other materials, how heavily it is rolled and for what length of time, how closely the grass is cut, etc.

A comparison between the relative strengths of the two teams can often suggest what kind of pitch would serve the interests of the home team best. Looking back to the golden days when the Oval team, Surrey, ruled the roost year in year out, one should not overlook Bert's (non-intervening) contribution!

13 A Shiver or a Crunch

We have said how everything began with a Big Bang. But what will be the ultimate fate of the Universe?

As the Universe expands and the galaxies move away from each other, their speeds of recession tend to slow down with time. This is because gravity tries to hold things together, and each galaxy is pulling on its neighbours through gravitational attraction.

But the strength of a gravitational force depends on the distance over which it operates; the bigger the distance, the weaker the force. The average separation between the galaxies increases with the expansion. So this in turn means that the strength of the slowing-down force is progressively diminishing,

The 64,000 dollar question is whether or not gravity is able to bring the expansion to a halt before its strength peters out completely. The long-term future of the Universe is governed by the answer to that question.

And that answer depends on how much matter there is in the Universe. Clearly, the greater the density of matter, the stronger will be the slowing-down force. There will, therefore, be a certain critical density of matter such that above that value, the expansion will one day stop; below that value, it will not.

Thus, we are faced with two possibilities:

POSSIBLE FATE NUMBER I

Suppose there *is* sufficient matter to halt the expansion. The galaxies come to a standstill. What happens next?

Although the galaxies are no longer moving, they continue to exert their gravitational force on each other. This means the galaxies will remain at rest only momentarily. No sooner have they stopped, than they start to move *towards* each other. Slowly at first, they gradually pick up speed. Eventually they come crashing together – to give a Big Crunch. Everything squashed down to a point! Ugh!

What happens after that?

Well, that might simply be *it*. Nothing more. The end of the Universe.

Or it might not. The alternative is that the Big Crunch would be followed by a Big Bounce. The whole process of expansion would then start all over again.

If that is the case, then we need to reassess the role of the Big Bang. So far we have regarded it as marking the moment of creation – an event of unique significance. But if this second scenario is correct, it could well be that the Big Bang was merely the most recent of a whole succession of Big Bounces.

How many Big Bounces could there have been? Who is to know? No information about previous states of the Universe can be passed on through a Big Bounce. Presumably the Big Bounces could have been going on indefinitely – and are destined to continue into the future without end.

Note also that if there is anything to this conjecture, then not only did the Big Bang not mark the creation of the Universe, it did not mark the beginning of time either – again contrary to

what was said earlier. There would have to have been time before the Big Bang in order to accommodate the earlier Big Bounces.

I should perhaps mention that one of the difficulties with this Big Bouncing idea is that no one has yet come up with a suggestion as to what might be the origin of the repulsive force needed to convert the inrush of material into an expansion. But then again, we do not understand why the Universe is expanding anyway.

A Universe that has always been bouncing, and will continue to bounce for ever, would be another way of getting rid of the naive idea of a Creator God who simply lights the blue touch-paper. If the Universe has *always* existed, then it did not require God to *bring* it into existence.

However, the idea of God the Sustainer is still relevant. God would remain the ground of all being, the ultimate reason why there had always been a Universe rather than nothing. His creativity would still be at work throughout all time.

POSSIBLE FATE NUMBER 2

What if the density is *less* than the critical value?

The expansion will go on for ever. The stars work through their life cycles, eventually using up all their fuel, the final fate of the star depending on how heavy it is:

The smaller ones simply fizzle out. Any accompanying planets they might have are then left cold and lifeless.

Medium-sized stars, like the sun, pass through something called 'the red giant stage'. They become bloated in size, changing colour from yellowy white to red. When this happens to the Sun, the Earth will sizzle. That will be the end of us – or at least the end of our descendants. (It's not due to happen for several thousands of millions of years, so don't panic!) Thereafter, the Sun will contract and cool down, leaving the Earth a cold cinder.

The larger stars in their old age blow up as supernovae, leaving behind a dense core of matter. If heavy enough, the core will collapse down to form a black hole. Black holes are sources of incredibly strong gravitational attraction, sucking in everything that comes close, even light itself – hence the name. Black holes give off a very weak form of radiation, such that eventually, over a very, very long period of time, they completely evaporate away – like a puddle on a hot day.

So there we have it: An ever-expanding Universe of frozen matter and weak radiation, quite incapable of any longer being able to support life. This is the so-called 'heat death' of the Universe.

AND THE WINNER IS . . .

'Right,' you will be asking, 'which one is it to be: graunch or brrr?'

If one looks up at the heavens and makes an inventory of everything one can see up there – the stars, the gases between the stars, the various forms of radiation – it all adds up to a density of about one tenth the critical value. Ah, so there's not enough to halt the expansion; it will go on for ever.

But wait. A recount has been ordered. What we have added up is all the stuff we *know* about. But we are constantly making fresh discoveries – coming across additional things out there that we hadn't previously thought about or noticed. With further developments in detecting equipment, who can possibly say what future discoveries will be made? And note, every new finding will *add* to the density, taking it ever closer to the magic critical value.

In fact, there is something very suspicious about getting a value of the density that is within a factor of only ten of the critical value.

'*Only* ten?' you ask.

In most situations in life, to be out by a factor of ten is to have missed by a mile. (Try persuading your bank manager to allow you to live at a level of expenditure that is ten times your salary!)

But here it is different. One could conceive of a universe in which the density of matter, compared to the critical density, could have been out by a factor of a million, or a billion, or a trillion, or – whatever the next one up from a trillion might be. It might have been bigger or smaller by such a factor. So to be within a factor of only ten is amazingly close.

So close, the suspicion is that the density probably exactly *equals* the critical value. How come? Perhaps early on in the Big Bang there was some mechanism at work such that it actually *ensured* that the density came out equal to the critical value.

Indeed, we now think we understand what that mechanism was. Recall how earlier we briefly mentioned that the Universe is thought to have initially undergone a super-rapid period of expansion – or inflation – prior to the 'normal' type of expansion taking over. One of the characteristics of the particular type of inflation envisaged is that, regardless of whatever the density was at earlier stages, by the end of the period of inflation the density would have adjusted itself to the critical value. In other words by the time inflation has done its job, the Universe has been fine-tuned to carry on expanding forever – but only just; the galaxies will come to a standstill in the infinite future.

WEATHER OUTLOOK – CONTINUING COLD

The thought that the Universe is destined to suffer a heat death fills some people with foreboding. It was this chilly prospect that was one of the reasons why, in the Epilogue to *The First Three Minutes*, Steven Weinberg was moved to make his remark about the Universe seeming pointless to him.

If all there is to reality is this physical world and the life it supports, then one would be bound to agree with him. It all does look a waste of time; it achieves nothing in the long run.

But that is not the Christian belief. According to the Christian way of looking at things, this physical life is but part of the story. The life we lead here is to be seen as but a process whereby spiritual beings come into existence. Through the cut and thrust of living out physical lives, spiritual beings develop and take shape. As they grow, so they begin to share in eternal life.

In time, a person's physical life comes to an end. But physical death is not the end of that person's existence. There remains that other type of existence: eternal life. Thus, those who once lived here, go on to some other form of life.

The adoption of such a view completely alters one's perspective. This Universe is not the be all and end all. The physical world is but a mould for shaping what really has value – our spiritual selves.

To adopt once more a sculpting metaphor: once the bronze sculpture has been cast, who needs the plaster mould any more? Indeed, the value of the sculpture is enhanced if, after it has done its job and fulfilled its purpose, the mould is deliberately broken. This ensures that what has been produced has the additional attraction of being a limited edition!

14 The Gurus Have Spoken

WHERE EINSTEIN GOT IT WRONG

Underpinning most of what I have told you about modern cosmology is Einstein's General Theory of Relativity. It was he who provided the framework for tackling big questions about space, time and the Universe. No wonder, for us physicists, Einstein is our hero. Many of us have photos of him pinned up on our office and laboratory walls – doubtless in the hope that something of his genius might rub off on us! (My own photo of him is full-length and life-size; I'm still waiting for it to work.)

But he's not everyone's cup of tea. That much is clear from the mail I receive whenever I am called upon to explain an aspect of Einstein's theory on TV.

I have grown especially wary of letters that begin: 'I am not a physicist, but . . .'

Invariably this leads to the assertion that Einstein got it all wrong. This is often coupled with an accusation that the physics establishment is wilfully ignoring or suppressing the views of the writer. Enclosed with the letter there is usually a paper, about half-a-dozen pages long, badly typed and with numerous crossings out. Its aim is to expose Einstein's mistake.

A casual look at the first couple of paragraphs is generally sufficient to reveal that the writer hasn't really understood the theory. I discreetly file it away unanswered. Painful experience has shown that it simply does not do to reply; it only lets your correspondent know they have managed to get through to you. Once you've made *that* mistake, they never stop writing.

In so discarding the letter, I hope against hope that I have not thereby inadvertently crushed the aspirations of a true genius! It is then I turn to answering the more 'sensible' letters.

ON A PEDESTAL

Of course, would-be critics of Einstein are in the minority. Generally speaking, I find people regard us scientists almost with a sense of awe. I sometimes reckon we could say the most utter rubbish on any subject we like, and still be guaranteed a respectful hearing.

Not so a theologian. While most people are only too willing to confess their total ignorance of science, and will believe anything a scientist will tell them, everyone – and I do mean *everyone* – is an expert when it comes to God! No one thinks twice before taking an Archbishop's views to task.

Now, don't get me wrong. I am quite happy that people should feel free to express their views about theological matters, even if they might be ill-informed. At least it shows they are interested in the subject.

The problem arises when a *scientist*, writing a science book, comes to his final chapter and decides to conclude with a few comments on philosophical or theological topics. We have in the course of this book come across Weinberg's comment about the Universe being 'pointless'; Hawking seeing 'no place for a Creator', and then going on to talk about 'knowing the Mind of God'.

The problem with these asides, casually tossed out, is that they assume a significance they often do not merit. They are seized upon by the media. Readers who might not have understood the science that went before, *do* understand what the author is saying here. And it is a *scientist* who is saying it, so everyone had better pay attention!

But in truth such philosophical comments ought to be prefaced by the phrase: 'I am not a theologian, but . . .'

Then we would know where we stood – and how much credence to place on the views that follow. No matter how great an authority someone might be in his chosen field, it is all too easy for him to find himself hopelessly out of his depth in some other area of expertise.

Nigel Hawkes, in a recent article in *The Times*, put it well:

Scientific superstars are not simply scientists writ large; they are gurus, prophets, and spiritual guides. As such, they have taken on a role that may be beyond their competence, or anybody else's.

HANDS ACROSS THE DIVIDE

What is so tantalizing is that some of the most fascinating questions do span the science/religion divide. In assessing the significance and implications of scientific developments in regard to the nature and dignity of humankind, one has clearly to venture beyond the safe bounds of pure science alone. The interaction between science and religion offers a whole range of interesting issues to be explored.

Given that there are pitfalls lying in wait for the unwary individual who would hazard beyond his or her own sphere of expertise, how can progress be made with these cross-disciplinary subjects?

As I see it, there has to be an exchange of ideas between experts in the different fields. Each participant must learn to respect the expertise of the other, and accept that the other's experience and background has fitted him or her for the type of investigation best suited to approaching the questions raised in that other field. The emphasis must be on *collaboration* and the free exchange of ideas.

Happily, this is now very much in evidence. For example, I was recently sent a large book, an inch and a half thick, entitled *Who's Who in Theology and Science*. It is the first edition of a 'user's guide' to those scientists, clergy and others currently active in the dialogue between science and theology. It lists the names of 1,000 people from 41 countries, together with 72 institutions, organizations and journals. Phew! before receiving this tome, I hadn't realized there were now so many of us working in this field. It must surely be one of the fastest-growing academic areas today.

All of this might surprise you. It is a fallacy commonly held that scientists, by their very nature, have a tendency to be atheistic. This simply is not true – at least, it is no more true of scientists than it is of people in any other walk of life.

The way I see it, most people seem to go through life for ever sitting on the fence when it comes to belief in God. It's not that they are antagonistic to religion. It's just that they never get around to doing anything about it. Tomorrow will do, and if not tomorrow then the tomorrow after that – until eventually there are no more tomorrows.

But if like me, you are in a profession that requires you to spend your whole working life pitting your mind against the deepest mysteries of the nature of space, time, matter and the cosmos, one can hardly avoid taking the next short step, which is to ask 'Why . . .?' – 'Why is it all here?' 'What's it all about?'

So what I find is that scientists, as a general rule, do not content themselves with sitting on the fence. They come off it – one way or the other. Thus, among the ranks of scientists you will find militant atheists, but also equally committed believers. With us, it tends to be all or nothing.

COUNTER-ATTACK

The trouble is that for too long, it has been the atheistic scientists who seem to have been most vociferous in their views, and the more effective in getting those views across to the public. How else is one to account for the fact that when the words 'science' and 'religion' are mentioned in the same breath, for most people the next word that comes to mind is 'conflict'?

When I first became involved in expressing my views about

science and religion, mostly through going round talking to schools, and occasionally getting an article published in a newspaper, it was a lonely business. Talk about a voice crying in the wilderness! Happily, all that is now changing – evidenced by that new *Who's Who*.

But that is only one sign of the changing times. Recently Science and Religion Forum celebrated its 20th anniversary. This is a group of about 200 scientists, clergy and laypeople who meet to discuss the insights science and religion can offer each other.

Then there is the Society of Ordained Scientists. Did you know that in the UK alone, between 50 and 60 scientists have given up their jobs to go into the ordained ministry – sufficient to form their own organization? I remember in particular a one-time research student of my own who gave up a highly paid, tax-free job in the big high-energy physics laboratory in Geneva, to take a position as a humble curate on one-sixth his former salary.

I am myself sometimes asked whether I have ever considered going into the full-time ordained ministry. I have thought about it – often – but have never really felt called to it. I prefer to remain a scientist and work as a layperson – a Reader in the Church of England.

Looking to the USA, one finds the 2,500-strong American Scientific Affiliation, 'founded out of concern for the relationship between science and Christian faith' and whose members are those 'who have made a personal commitment of themselves and their lives to Jesus Christ as Lord and Saviour, and who have made a personal commitment of themselves and their lives to a scientific description of the world'.

At Princeton there is the Center of Theological Inquiry, a new research establishment, founded with the prime aim of bringing theology into line with modern thought and particularly with modern scientific thought. On the West Coast, at Berkeley in California, there is the Center for Theology and Natural Science, with its vigorous programme of research, lecture courses and conferences.

Publications abound in the field; journals, individual books, as well as a series entitled *Theology and Science at the Frontiers of Knowledge*.

And so one could go on. All heartening signs of the growing *collaboration* that is now taking place between experts in different fields. I only wish more people *knew* such activities were going on. Perhaps then they would be better able to assess the value of the casual, ill-considered comments of atheistic scientists.

WEEKENDS AT WINDSOR

Let me illustrate this process of collaboration by citing my own experience of the way an individual can gain from interaction with others.

In 1983 I received a request to attend a weekend at St George's House, Windsor Castle. The Duke of Edinburgh had become interested in exploring the relationship between religion and psychology – particularly Jungian psychology. Theologians and psychologists had already held one weekend meeting with him. On that occasion the view had been expressed that they ought to involve one or two scientists next time. That's how I came to be invited to their second gathering.

There were about thirty of us, including spouses. The inclusion of the spouses somewhat surprised me, especially as they were expected to attend the three prepared lectures, and also the discussion groups that followed each lecture, together with the plenary session at the end. But then I realized what a shrewd move this was. The presence of the spouses was a constant reminder to everyone not to use incomprehensible jargon, and to keep all explanations simple – something that was not only required for the spouses but for *all* in attendance when the subject was not the one in which they were personally expert.

The first session I attended was exceptionally lively. The speaker was Peter Atkins, a physical chemist from Oxford. He gave a stinging attack on religion. He contrasted the way the statements of science were open to verification, whereas religion depended on faith – faith being the acceptance of that which could not be proven. This, I knew, was old hat. (I explained why in Chapter 7, if you remember.) So what was Atkins playing at?

'Ah! I know. It's a Devil's advocate talk to stir us up,' I thought. I often do the same sort of thing myself when asked to speak to schools or at clergy training sessions. I call my talk *Thirty Ways Science Disproves Religion*. That takes up the first half-hour; in the second half-hour, I show what was wrong with all those arguments.

Atkins, having trotted out his old verification chestnut, next ruled out 'Why . . .?'-type questions; we were only to address 'How . . .?'-type questions. (Concede that one, and poor old God doesn't get a look in.)

What I particularly admired about Atkins' approach was the way each time he referred to science, he spoke of it in the same terms as a religious believer might use when addressing God. He would speak in awed, hushed tones of the omnipotence and majesty of science, for example. Clever that. I made a mental note to do the same myself in future.

But then I grew uneasy. I looked at my watch; he was more than half-way through his allotted time. If he was not careful he would not leave himself sufficient time to 'put things right'. Still he went on . . . and on: 'There is nothing that cannot be understood . . . there is nothing that cannot be explained . . . everything is extraordinarily simple . . .'

Then he stopped. That was it; he had finished. To my complete astonishment, and that of others, it dawned on us that it had *not* been a Devil's advocate talk at all. He actually *believed* this!

The discussion that followed was intense – to put it mildly. Prince Philip began by seeking clarification as to why the lecturer had concentrated exclusively on 'How . . .?'-type questions.

'What about the 'Why . . .?'-type questions?' he asked.

'You can't ask those questions,' was the abrupt reply.

'Why ever not?!'

'Because they are meaningless,' declared Atkins as though it were obvious.

The Prince looked dumbfounded.

In the discussion groups next day, what most seemed to interest the psychologists present was what I had noticed myself about the way Atkins had spoken of science as though it were some kind of God. They explained that whereas Freudian psychology makes the claim that religion is a manifestation of an unhealthy neurosis, in Jungian psychology, religion is absolutely central to the mature, well-balanced life. If the religious drive does not find its normal method of expression, then it will manifest itself in other ways. Atkins had provided a classic example of someone creating a substitute God.

Although strenuous efforts were made throughout to keep the discussion accessible to the non-expert, time and again I found myself getting lost. The psychologists kept speaking of 'archetypes' and the 'collective unconscious', and I did not know what these meant. I also noticed that they seemed to refer to the 'self' in a rather specialized way.

As the weekend drew to a close, I asked one of them how I might make good my lack of background in the subject. I was given the titles of various books. These I dutifully read before the next meeting.

This was held four months later. At that meeting I was delighted to discover that I could now follow most of the psychological discussion.

At the meeting after that, it was my turn to deliver one of the set lectures. I decided to chance my arm and include some reference to psychology. I did so keeping an anxious eye out for any signs of the psychologists having fits of apoplexy.

In the event, they were very kind to me. One of them discreetly came up to me afterwards and said, 'That was very interesting, but there was one point where you said "archetype". I'm pretty sure you meant "archetypal image". Yes?' I hurried away to consult my books and find out what the distinction might be!

At subsequent meetings, we invited philosophers to join in our discussions. That gave me a chance to try out some philosophical allusions in my later lectures.

As time went on I began to see interesting parallels between the various fields. I felt that all this ought to be brought together and written up. But how? How would it be possible to span so wide a field as would include theology, physics, psychology, biology, philosophy and social anthropology.

A CHANGE OF SCENE

Then in 1986 I first heard about the newly established Center of Theological Inquiry at Princeton. I had a year's sabbatical leave due, when I would be free of all teaching commitments. Normally such time would be spent on uninterrupted research work. I decided instead to apply to the Center, stating that I wanted to write a book based on the outcome of the St George's House discussions. I was delighted to be accepted.

For a whole year I mixed with theologians, philosophers and psychologists, as well as scientists. I set to and wrote *Grounds for Reasonable Belief* (Scottish Academic Press, 1989). I managed to persuade no less than eighteen academics to read and comment on its various drafts. Whatever merit there might have been in that book, it was largely thanks to them.

It was a tough business. There was one particularly blunt character at the Center at that time. If he felt you were waffling or not explaining yourself clearly, he would brutally cut in with 'What's your point?'

As a well-mannered Englishman, it took me a while to get used to this American brusqueness, and to realize that no offence was meant.

I will always remember one episode. I had written something about the nature of mind. I showed it to one of the philosophers.

'It's manifestly obvious you have not read Ryle's *Concept of Mind*. Go away and read it, then we shall discuss it,' he ordered.

I slunk out of his office feeling like a schoolboy who had not done his homework – and thinking to myself, 'Why didn't I stick to my physics?'

But I read the book – and was over the Moon. I found there

some wonderful supporting evidence for a point I had been trying to establish. Next morning I could not wait for my colleague to come in. When he arrived, I blurted it all out in an excited torrent. He simply sat there smiling.

'Yes,' he eventually replied. 'I thought you'd enjoy it. Now I need you to help *me*. I want you to explain quantum theory . . .'

That's how collaboration goes. That's how progress is made in these interdisciplinary areas. In particular, that is how the science/religion dialogue *should* be conducted. It should *not* consist of scientists tossing out ill-digested sound-bites at the end of their popular science books.

If they feel moved to draw some philosophical or theological lesson from the science, that's fair enough. But they owe it to themselves, and to their readers, to at least take the trouble to try out those ideas on experts in those fields before rushing into print.

Theology is a field of study demanding as much diligence, thoroughness and integrity as any other subject. It deserves the same measure of respect as science.

Postscript
True, But Is It News?

You might recall that at the time I began writing this book I was rather dreading an encounter with Dr Richard Dawkins.

The Sunday before our scheduled clash, *The Observer* reminded its readers of its former article describing how Dawkins had 'demolished' the Archbishop of York in the earlier science/religion debate at Edinburgh. This did nothing for my nerves!

However, when the day of the debate came and I found myself walking the short stretch from Green Park underground station to Carlton House Terrace, where the Royal Society is based, I felt better in the knowledge that many of my friends at church had said that they would be remembering me in their prayers that evening.

On entering the elegant, imposing building I first met up with Sir Hermann Bondi – a genial, warm-hearted humanist. He had been teamed up with Dawkins. Next to arrive was my team-mate, Hugh Montefiore, the retired Bishop of Birmingham. A tall patrician figure, he looked a little lost in this, the heart of the scientific establishment. As he explained to me, he'd had no training in science, and was rather at a loss to understand why he had been asked to take part in the event.

Then there entered 'the dapper Dr Dawkins', as *The Observer* had described him. It was the first time I had met him. I was immediately struck with how bronzed and good-looking he was – at least, I reckoned women would think him so. I found myself wondering, somewhat incongruously, why he had not made a career in films. That way he wouldn't have been causing me all this hassle!

On being introduced to each other by one of the organizers, Dawkins straight away declared how much he had enjoyed my *Uncle Albert* books. He actually enjoyed them! I immediately thought that anyone who enjoyed Uncle Albert couldn't be all that bad, could they?

But wait. Was this a trick to lull me into a false sense of security, an attempt to put me off my guard before he launched his 'withering attacks' (as the newspaper had described his earlier debating style)? But there was no time to ponder on this. With the arrival of the chairman of the session, the physics professor and author of *The Mind of God*, Paul Davies, who had flown in from Australia for the occasion, we trooped into the hall to take up our positions on the platform.

ALL RIGHT ON THE NIGHT

As it turned out, I needn't have worried. The debate was conducted in a constructive and courteous manner – not a bit like the reported confrontation at Edinburgh. I was able to get across many of the points I have now made in this book. Montefiore added his carefully considered theological insights. Bondi sided with Dawkins over their lack of belief in God, but tended to join forces with Montefiore and myself in affirming the dignity of human beings against the tendency to regard humans as *merely* a form of evolved animal.

I was left wondering why this debate, unlike the other, had proceeded so smoothly. Perhaps it was due to skilful chairmanship by Davies; I knew he had been anxious for us to avoid the aggro that had marred the previous debate. Was it because the discussion largely centred on the ramifications of the Big Bang theory, and so was centred on physics, rather than on evolution and genetics – zoologist Dawkins' own line of specialism? Possibly it had something to do with the way I managed to get in quick with a remark that I knew of no one who had come to know God by looking for him in the gaps between what science could currently explain – looking for some piece of scientific data that would prove he existed. That was entirely the wrong approach, I said – knowing from the newspaper report that this line of argument had been precisely how Dawkins had managed to side-track the earlier discussion in Edinburgh. Or then again, perhaps it had something to do with the prayers being offered?

This is not to say that the debate lacked tension. Far from it. There were cut-and-thrust exchanges, and out-and-out disagreement on various issues. But there was no acrimony, no cheap point-scoring.

To underline just how good-humoured the debate had been, the participants adjourned afterwards to a restaurant for a pleasant supper together! I sat next to Dawkins and thoroughly enjoyed his company.

Towards the end of the meal, Montefiore and I had to leave a little before the others, to catch our respective trains. As we emerged from the restaurant, he said, 'Well, Russell, I think we can say that went quite well.'

Then he took me by the arm and added, 'But thank God you were there!'

With that he abruptly turned on his heel and strode off into the night.

NO NEWS IS . . .

And what of the press coverage of the event? What did the reporters make of it all? We knew that at the very least *The Mail, The Telegraph, the Guardian* and *The Independent* had sent representatives. Over the next few days I spent a small fortune buying up all these papers. It is not that I expected headlines – 'Christians Give Lions a Mauling' – or anything like that. But I did expect *something*.

But not a word. Not a dickey-bird! It was as though the event had never happened. Even *The Observer*, which had played so prominent a part in whipping up interest in the debate beforehand, remained totally silent.

It is not often I write to newspapers. In fact, I can't recall having done so more than once or twice in my lifetime. But I did write to the Editor of *The Observer* that week:

Sir,

Under the gleeful headline 'God Comes a Poor Second before the Majesty of Science', your science correspondent reported (on Easter Sunday of all days) how Richard Dawkins 'inflicted grievous intellectual harm' on the Archbishop of York in a debate on science and religion. We were told of 'smugly smiling atheists' and 'Lions 10; Christians nil'.

In your 17th May issue, the same writer relished the prospect of a forthcoming debate entitled 'Has Science Eliminated the Need for God?', in which 'the stakes will increase when Dawkins together with Sir Hermann Bondi take up cudgels – at the Royal Society – against the Right Reverend Hugh Montefiore and Russell Stannard.'

Why was there no subsequent account of how this second debate went? Could it be that the outcome of the replay was not to your correspondent's liking? Being myself one of the protagonists it is not for me to pronounce on the final score. All I will say is that I couldn't help noticing religious believers leaving the hall with broad grins. And, let's not forget, away goals count double!

Yours
Professor Russell Stannard

The letter was not published – make what you will of that. The two articles *The Observer* did publish, presenting as they did a completely one-sided view of the state of play in the science/religion dialogue, were left to do their damage.

For a few days I was indignant, but then I brushed the matter aside; there was nothing more I could do. To be honest, I couldn't altogether blame *The Observer*, or the other newspapers.

'God Gets His P45', as *The Mail* recently trumpeted in a headline, is news. It's not *true*, but it would have been news if it had been true. And it sells newspapers.

'God is alive and well, and is still in charge' is true; but it is not news.

No, it's not *news*; it is *Good News* – and that is something altogether different.

Index

anthropic principle 88–104, 108

background radiation 11–14
Bible 17–24, 114–19
Big Bang 8–16, 27–30, 36–38, 54, 89, 102

creation from nothing 55–58
creation of space 30
creation of time 36–38

elements in the Universe 14–15, 89–93
evolution 17–19, 93, 101
expansion of the Universe 10–11, 27–30, 102, 125–31

freewill 50–53

galaxies 8–11

God, the Creator 39–45
  his foreknowledge 49–53
  his Mind 121–24

Heaven 45–47

laws of nature 61–71

mathematics 64–71
mind 81–87, 120–23
miracles 111–24

other intelligent forms of life 25–26

quantum theory 58–60

relativity theory 30–37, 69

science, its limitations 77–87
spacetime 34–38, 48–52

Theory of Everything 62–80

verification principle 74–77, 139